Roll the Windows Down, It's Raining:

And Other Lessons I Learned from My Father and Son

by Nicholas Lore

Jebaire Publishing, LLC
Snellville, GA

Roll the Windows Down, It's Raining:
  And Other Lessons I learned from My Father and Son

ISBN-10: 0-9786796-5-2
ISBN-13: 978-0-9786796-5-1
Library of Congress Control Number: 2010928041

Supervising Editor: Shannon Clark
Cover Design: Jebaire Publishing
Cover photo provided by Nick Lore (of son Andrew)

Visit Nick Lore's website at:
www.nicklore.com

Visit Jebaire's website at:
www.jebairepublishing.com

Dedication

After a lot of thought about a lot of exceptional people that influenced my life, I decided to dedicate this book to my third grade (both years) remedial reading and writing teacher Mrs. Vinegar. She was the epitome of compassion. She taught us strugglers not to confuse our learning challenges with our self-worth. When the difficulties appeared insurmountable, Mrs. Vinegar would be there to remind me: "Nicky, many things will be difficult for you, but you are special; God doesn't make junk."

Author Nick Lore

Table of Contents

Foreword

A big part of life is about making choices. In fact, every day we are faced with numerous decisions. Sometimes we make good choices; sometimes our choices lead to heartache and pain. In this ground-breaking book author Nick Lore comes to terms with some of his wayward choices in a dramatic way.

Like many men in the hectic world of business, Nick was carving out a successful career, climbing the corporate ladder, earning good money. During a 20 year period his life consisted of punishing travel schedules, constant deadlines and the challenge of consistently hitting financial targets. It cost him his marriage, a statistic shared by many in today's world of ego-driven consumerism and the never-ending search for "success".

Sometimes life gives us a wake up call when we least expect it. If we are tuned in, we respond. If not, we go blindly on creating even worse circumstances. Nick's wake up was a diagnosis of prostate cancer. That's something you don't ignore unless you're planning for a much shorter life than you originally anticipated.

As you'll discover, Nick's "light bulb moment" totally changed his perspective about life. "What are my most important priorities?" he asked himself. That's a question a lot of men need to think about.

Here's another: "When I'm in my senior years, will my greatest memory be about the number of boardroom meetings I attended, or will it be focused on the unique memorable experiences I created and shared with the people I love, especially my family?"

Nick made a big decision when he chose the latter option. This book tells the story of his 15 month odyssey that he shared primarily with his young son, Andrew. His writing is clear, candid and inspiring! As he vividly paints pictures of his childhood memories and ensures Andrew gets to relive them, you'll feel like you are right there alongside them both. Each new experience contains important life lessons that will help every father who reads this to become a wonderful role model for his children. These are expertly summarized at the end of the book.

As my wife Fran, who is also a skillful writer, says: "Too many people today are missing out on life playing the When—Then game. When I make enough money, then I'll be happy; when we buy a bigger home, then we'll have more time to relax; when I finish this big project, then I'll have time for the kids."

The When—Then game is a trap many fathers have fallen into. Nick Lore will show you how to climb out of that trap and live a life of faith-based significance. His story is timely and essential reading for fathers everywhere. It will make you rethink your priorities. More importantly, it will give you the opportunity to be the father your children would love you to be.

Les Hewitt
Author, *The Power of Focus*

Acknowledgments

In early 2002, right after my cancer diagnosis, I read The Power of Focus by Les Hewitt, Mark Victor Hansen and Jack Canfield. Impressed with the book's life changing potential, I called Les. Our telephone conversation led to a rewarding visit with Les' impressive family and associates in Calgary, Canada. We stayed in touch, and later I brought Les to Alabama and Georgia to conduct seminars for my sales people and their Realtor and builder clients. Les was a big hit with everyone.

When Les learned of my journaled 15-month adventure with my son Andrew, he asked if he could read the journal. He did and offered the following: "You are a good editor away from a good book." Les, for that encouragement I will be forever thankful.

Les's subsequent referral to his capable editor Rod Chapman started out on an interesting note after I emailed him the manuscript. Quite seriously Rod inquired: "What have you got here?" When I assured him there was a book in there somewhere, his out loud thought was a dubious: "Really?" We agreed on the terms of the editing agreement and Rod started the process of carving through 150,000 words to find 75,000 or so that might indeed become the book Les envisioned. I thank you Rod for your editorial mastery.

Brittany Vincente, it is our secret how much you did before Les and Rod saw the manuscript. All of your work and encouragement is much appreciated.

My computer wiz neighbor and friend George Sipe was there with me all along the way for computer and related issues. He modestly downplayed his contributions as I oft thanked God for his every involvement. Thank you, George.

There were many who encouraged and prayed me though the obstacles including the rejections. They include Pam Jones Bewac, Fred Wirt, Mike Manness, Melissa Hoggatt and my wife, Mandy. Pam was also an invaluable help in developing our Family and Friends mailing list for this book.

There would be no book were it not for the three wonderful people that have so richly blessed my life with love, forgiveness, and humor well beyond the norm. I thank God daily for the blessings of family and most especially for my children Dawn, Kim, and Andrew.

I thank God that he chose this ADHD, Dyslexic who spent two years in 3rd grade and barely passed the rest to write a pretty good book to highlight His love even for, perhaps especially for, the least of us.

Martin Deacon, thank you for hand-delivering my manuscript to Multnomah's executive editor David Kopp. David, it was your caring advice that led me to Jebaire Publishing.

Finally to Shannon Clark and the rest of the good folks at Jebaire Publishing, thank you for reaching out to that pariah of the publishing industry, the dreaded first time author.

We will praise Him for every life that Roll the Windows Down, It's Raining touches.

Prologue

IN CRISIS, A MESSAGE

There is no such thing as chance;
And what to us seems merest accident,
Springs from the deepest source of destiny.

-- Johann Schiller

Fascinated by the rising tide's wonderful hydraulic commotion below the train trestle spanning Greynolds Park waterway, I failed to hear the frantic shouting of my father. Finally the sound of frenzied horn-blowing demanded my attention. Aghast, I looked up to see a Southeast Railroad locomotive bearing down on me.

In an instant as the freight train roared past I made the decision not to jump. Frozen with fear, a torrent of air currents battering me, I fought interminably to hold on against the mighty train's stormy fluxes, afraid that I would lose my grip and be sucked unmercifully into the thundering wheels, or that I would be hurled carelessly into the shallow, turbulent water laden with jagged oyster shells.

As the last freight car clattered past, I looked south toward Miami wondering how the train had missed crushing my six-year-old body.

Sitting in exhausted disbelief, I looked at my father. Our eyes met for a long, bewildered moment.

The joys of catching the rising early-morning tide and enough Blue Crab for dinner had vanished with the train. My father was a quiet, unassuming and stoic man who very much loved his family but rarely showed outright affection. He purposefully gathered the crab nets and baited lines that he had tossed in the rising tide only minutes before, and returned them to the trunk of our car. Lost for words, we drove home knowing that I had been spared a dreadful death. After twenty minutes of silence, he finally found his voice.

"Nicky, you could have been killed back there."

"I know, Dad," I said apologetically. "I'm sorry."

"This proves God has a special purpose for you," my father's final words on the matter burned indelibly in my brain. "Today He spared your life."

Dad lived for more than forty years after that fateful morning, yet he never again mentioned the train incident. Driving back, there was no desire for celebration, only a profoundly humble appreciation. From that unforgettable experience I came to understand that no father should know the sorrow of losing a child, and that every child desires the love and direction of a caring dad. I began to understand that life is more than a random series of events.

Today, that understanding still forms the foundation of my faith.

Chapter One

AN ABUNDANT LIFE

What you see and hear depends a good deal on where you are standing: it also depends on what sort of person you are.

-- C.S. Lewis

Wealth in a Loving Family

In 1942 during the heat of the Second World War Corporal Louis Lore was sent to further his Army training at Ft. Benning in Columbus, Georgia. It was an interim stop before receiving orders to report to Dover, England. A month before leaving for Dover, he ventured a bus trip to Newnan, Georgia, some eighty miles north, where he met a southern belle who he later told me was the most beautiful girl he'd ever seen.

Dad never stopped feeling that way about Mom. They were an unlikely couple – a first-generation American Italian boy from Brooklyn and a small-town Georgia lass brought together by a world war – but fifteen months later they were married. They had three children. I was named Nicholas after my paternal grandfather, my brother Robert was named after our maternal granddad, and my sister Mary received the name of our paternal grandmother.

Dad died before Andrew was born, but he would have loved his sixth grandchild as much as he did the first five, including my two daughters, Dawn and Kimberly, from my first marriage.

Mom and Dad both attended my second marriage to Mandy Michelle Marshall in 1993 in Camden, South Carolina. They both wholeheartedly welcomed their new daughter into our family. It was Mandy's first marriage, and her parents wondered why she had decided to marry a man fifteen years her senior. I understood their concerns, but today I'm pleased to have a great relationship with Dr. Marshall and Nancy. They were particularly pleased when I fathered their first grandchild, Andrew, at the ripe old age of fifty-five.

How did a boy who grew up in South Florida meet a girl from South Carolina? We met in New York City, of course.

Mandy had lived in Manhattan for ten years before we were married. Two years before we met, I had received a promotion and moved to New York from Florida. We met at a DeMoss House social. The DeMoss family had a stately brownstone on the upper east side that they graciously opened to people who wanted to further their spiritual growth and foster friendships in the busy metropolis. One beautiful spring afternoon I asked Mandy if I could walk her home. On the way through Central Park I said I had been wondering if she was dating anyone. "Sort of," she responded.

I assured her that if she started dating me the same question would elicit a response infused with a great deal more certainty. Fifteen months later we were married in historic Bethesda Presbyterian Church. Designed by the first American-born architect, Robert Mills, and built in 1822, I was pleased that the church was older than me.

Before Mandy and I met, I'd already accepted a job offer to become a partner in a company in Atlanta. A month after we met I left for Atlanta, and from then on most of our courting consisted of me flying to Manhattan on business and staying the weekend, or Mandy visiting Atlanta. Fortunately, back then round-trip airfares between Atlanta and New York were only a hundred dollars.

After our marriage, we settled into an apartment in Dunwoody with a beautiful sixteenth- story view of the growing Atlanta skyline. My new partnership was a departure from my thirty-year career in retail mortgage banking. I became a loan sale advisor for the Resolution Trust Corporation. In this new role I used my seasoned customer list and sealed bid auctions advertised weekly in the Wall Street Journal to sell hundred-million-dollar pools of loans in the open market.

Resolution Trust Corporation (RTC) had emerged during the demise of the saving and loan industry. RTC gathered loans from failed S&Ls and sold them in auctions through loan sale advisors. This offset some of the losses of American taxpayers resulting from the S&L financial crisis of the early 1990s. I implemented creative ideas that made the sales more cost- and time-efficient. In little more than a year I managed to move over a billion dollars in mortgage loans, and I sold myself out of a job. I went back into retail mortgage banking for several years.

Mandy gave up her career so we could start a family. We lost two children in the womb before God blessed us with Andrew. Mandy's battle with hypothyroidism and my old-man status made us decide against having more children.

Today when people ask Andrew if he has brothers or sisters he beamingly affirms, "I have two sisters and a brother." By this he means my two grown daughters and my oldest daughter's husband, John. He looks forward to having a second brother when his sister Kimberly gets married.

Andrew has dishwater blond hair and beautiful blue eyes. With his wonderfully endearing smile he looks just like I did at his age. Mandy sometimes grows weary of people saying he looks just like his dad. Even worse, he often acts just like his dad. But the truth is that he is the new and much-improved version of me, with the rough edges smoothed out and many endearing new features. This, of course, is due to the Marshall gene pool.

Bold yet sensitive, Andrew is full of energy and ideas. When we take him to the park to play, which is often, we are fascinated by how easily he makes friends. There are no barriers, not even language, for our caring and gregarious son. He's just fun to be around. Andrew loves his family, broccoli, running, jumping, climbing, being read to, reading, listening to music and lots of other stuff, not necessarily in that order. He does not like oatmeal.

Just Like That

His eyes told me I would die soon. It was late spring. I had seen my last autumn.

- Eugene O'Kelly

At 53, Eugene O'Kelly was in the full swing of life. Chairman and CEO of one of the largest accounting firms in the United States, he had enjoyed a successful career and continued to draw happiness from his wife, children, family and close friends – until one day he was diagnosed with late-stage brain cancer and given three to six months to live. Just like that.

One Day at a Time

We don't determine the manner or time of our death, but we can determine how we shall live.

- Anon

More than fifty years after my near-death experience on the train trestle at Greynolds Park, I found myself driving to meet a doctor at a radiotherapy clinic in Atlanta, Georgia. After thirty weekly radiation treatments, a blood test six months later had revealed an unsettling rise in my PSA reading. If my prostate cancer was spreading, the only option would be chemotherapy.

More than dying, I was concerned about Andrew, who could soon be fatherless. I thought about how important it was to spend time with him. I knew I needed God's help to be the kind of man that He and I wanted Andrew to become. I knew, too, that I needed to make fewer mistakes with Andrew than I had with the girls. It was hurtful to recall how my pride and stupidity in an unhappy first marriage had caused my daughters from that marriage, Dawn and Kimberly, so much heartache.

I remembered the joy Mandy and I had felt when our son took his first breath. He had been in no hurry to leave the warm, nurturing environment of his mother's womb. After twenty exhausting hours of labor, we finally beheld the miracle we named Andrew in honor of the Apostle Peter's caring brother. We felt that our son, like his namesake, would mature into a servant leader. Cradling him in my arms I quietly, reverently reveled in the bliss of the birth of my third child – a child who was, interestingly, an uncle to my two grandchildren. I would soon tell people I loved my grandchildren so much that I decided to have one of my own.

Since being diagnosed with prostate cancer, I'd read enough to know that my hectic career including extended hours, heavy work-loads and too many high-fat business dinners had contributed to my condition. Wondering if my recent commitment to eating better, making time for rest and exercising regularly had come too late, I thought that it isn't quite true that we don't determine the manner or time of our death.

Entering the clinic's crowded parking lot, I thought about how peaceful and reflective people with near-death experiences feel as they pass from this life to the next. It felt as if I was having that kind of experience. The memories came easily. I remembered the easy times of my childhood in Miami. Memories of my mother and father cheering me on at football games and track meets, smiling with encouragement, flooded into my head. I knew they were proud of me. Their love motivated me to be my best, even though I grew up with Attention Deficit Hyper-activity Disorder (ADHD) and dyslexia at a time when these psychological challenges were undiagnosed and untreated. I knew the searing pain of feeling inadequate beyond all effort.

Because I was a special-needs child, I have come to understand that all children have special needs. More than anything else, children need to know that they are loved and valued. Sometimes I think the most disadvantaged children, the children with the most special needs, are those who live in big homes and ride around in luxury cars.

I am not suggesting there is something wrong with being wealthy. Many wealthy families have done especially well by their families and society. But when we have so much, the issue is a lack of contentment. Often, we misguidedly think that the pursuit of just a little more justifies postponing time with our loved ones. Most men have a commendable inherent desire to protect and provide for their families but success, like medicine, has the potential to become poison. The question of our age is this: "How much is enough?"

I began reflecting on the brevity of life, and the regret of missed opportunities. Missed opportunities and other forms of neglect often create a downward cycle. When a father fails his son, inevitably he also fails his grandson and his family and, ultimately, society. The far-reaching effects of his failure are daunting.

Harry Chapin's hit song *Cat's In The Cradle* poignantly portrays the downward generational spiral of fathers ignoring their sons. Every time I hear it I share the sorrow a son suffers when his father neglects meaningful time with him. The lyrics are about Harry's father and his son, but they also portray a growing generational affliction of misplaced priorities. The words forewarn of the seduction of affluence and influence. Chapin wrote these foreboding lyrics based on a poem by his wife, Sandy, who wrote of Harry's unhappy childhood. Harry wrote of being distraught over missing the birth of their son due to the demands of his touring. Chapin lamented his situation, but failed to break the cycle.

Cat's In The Cradle

My child arrived just the other day,
He came to the world in the usual way.
But there were planes to catch, and bills to pay,
He learned to walk while I was away.
And he was talkin' 'fore I knew it, and as he grew,
He'd say "I'm gonna be like you, yeh,
I know I'm gonna be like you".

(Chorus)
And the cat's in the cradle and the silver spoon,
Little Boy Blue and The Man In The Moon.
"When ya comin' home Dad?"
"I don't know when, we'll get together then, son,
Ya know we'll have a good time then".

Well my son turned 10 just the other day,
He said "Thanks for the ball Dad, come let's play.
Can ya teach me to throw?" I said
"Not today, I got a lot to do." He said "That's ok".
And then, he walked away but a smile never came,
He said "I'm gonna be like him, yeh,
Ya know I'm gonna be like him".

(Chorus)

Well he came from college just the other day,
So much like a man I just had to say
"Son I'm proud of you, can ya sit for a while?"
He shook his head, and he said with a smile
"What I'd really like Dad, is to borrow the car keys.
See ya later, can I have them please?"

(Chorus)

Well I've long since retired, my son's moved away,
I called him up just the other day.
I said "I'd like to see you, if you don't mind."
He said "I'd love to Dad, if I can find the time.
You see my new job's a hassle and the kids have the flu,
But it's sure nice talking to you Dad,
It's been sure nice talking to you."
And as he hung up the phone it occurred to me,
He'd grown up just like, my boy, was just like me.

- Harry Chapin

I am not assailing Harry Chapin. At least he recognized his problem before his untimely death. The song underscores how we can be physically alive yet spiritually and emotionally dead to those who love us and need us. It emphasizes the brevity of life and the importance of replacing impoverishing behavior with good habits. Deferring time with loved ones is one of the tragedies of recent generations. By our actions, too many of us have prioritized getting ahead and, incredibly, watching mind-numbing television over spending meaningful time with our families.

Sitting in the waiting room of the radiotherapy clinic, I thought about how just the day before Andrew had joyfully predicted that one day we would share the adventure of being train engineers. The test results would not render me as anxiously helpless as I had been on the trestle that fateful morning fifty years ago, but I was again reminded of how little control we have over our lives.

The waiting area was packed with men, some with their wives, waiting to see a physician. Others were waiting to be called for radiation treatment. It was clear that in the mutual affliction of cancer there is camaraderie. Fear of the unknown, fear of death, binds us together. Some of the men cried, some were angry and others were stoic. All were caught up in the hope of a cure. The talk in the clinic's busy waiting area was that chemotherapy would give me only two or three more years. I thought about how abruptly determining this office visit would be. I liked Dr. Critz's no-nonsense manner, but this would be one of the most starkly candid moments of my life.

Seeing the other afflicted men reminded me of how I had responded when I was first diagnosed with prostate cancer. I had called everyone I knew who had prostate cancer or who knew someone with it. My first call was to Pastor Frank Barker, who is a prostate cancer survivor. Frank and Barbara Barker are two of the finest people I know. Words are not adequate to describe the dynamics of their humble faith. They positively affect so many people in so many places all over the world that they are the embodiment of what the Apostle Paul called the fruit of the Spirit.

But the fruit of the Spirit is love, joy, peace, patience, gentleness, goodness, faith, meekness, temperance: against such there is no law.

- Galatians 5: 22 & 23

Worshipping and studying under the guidance of the Barkers was spiritually very rewarding. More than anything, I wanted the support of Frank and Barbara.

As I sat in the waiting area praying for a reversal of my life-threatening rising PSA levels, I remained contemplative and thankful that Mandy and my daughters had also prayed for me. I needed some good news. The prospects of dying from prostate cancer were frightening, but what most concerned me was Andrew. Every child needs a dad to help him realize his dreams. No matter what the blood test revealed, I vowed that I would make meaningful changes in my life. I would spend more time with my wife, with my adult children, with my grandchildren and especially with Andrew. If I didn't have long to live, at least I could make the best use of whatever time I did have.

Lost in thought, like that long-ago day on the trestle only vaguely did I hear the nurse calling my name. "Mr. Lore, you appear to be deep in thought."

We exchanged pleasantries as I followed her to the examination room. Dr. Frank Critz soon arrived and in his usual direct manner picked up my file, glanced at the PSA test and with a poker face announced the results.

"Mr. Lore, your PSA number has fallen."

My anxiety turned into unbridled joy. I wasn't out of the woods, but the declining number was a good sign. Dr. Critz reminded me that I needed to return for another blood test in six months. I shook the doctor's hand with heartfelt thankfulness. I had no desire to discuss the implications of a possible higher PSA reading six months from now. From now on it would be one day, and one appointment, at a time.

Eager to tell everyone my good news, from the car I called Mandy, Dawn, Kimberly and a few close friends like the Barkers to thank them for their prayers. On the way home I stopped at a quiet park. Sitting on a bench in meditative silence for I don't know how long, I basked gratefully in soothing fragrances carried on cool breezes.

Blessing in Disguise

The previous week we'd been told that Andrew would miss being eligible for kindergarten by six days. At the time this had seemed disruptive, an unwanted change in our plans. Mandy had been accepted into Mercer University graduate school. We couldn't interfere with Mandy's assistant teaching position, or her graduate school schedule. I would continue to be supportive of Mandy's studies. She was a good student and I knew she would earn her graduate degree and teacher's license. But I would make some changes to my own life. As I reflected, the situation with Andrew's kindergarten began to emerge as a blessing and an opportunity.

I would put my career on hold. Andrew and I would spend the next fifteen months sharing the joy of being together. Father and son, together we would visit the ocean, climb a mountain, ride the rails. I began to get excited about the possibilities. We would plan simple times that included family and friends. I would live my life more abundantly, knowing that God had again interceded. I would do my best to forge a father-son bond that would last a lifetime – and beyond.

Chapter Two

CHASING DAYLIGHT

*Loneliness and the feeling of being
unwanted is the most terrible poverty.*

- Mother Teresa

When I arrived home from the clinic that evening, I told Andrew one of his favorite bedtime stories. It is a true story.

After graduating from high school, I had enlisted in the United States Air Force and was soon stationed at Royal Air Force Base Chicksands in England. RAF Chicksands was surrounded by beautiful rolling farms including a pristine creek that flowed gracefully through the base. Chicksands was also home to a stately historic abbey that served as officer's quarters and came complete with a ghost. The latter, reported to be a nun, was of great interest to Andrew, especially at bedtime and most especially with the lights out!

 I arrived at the base late on a Friday, tired from my trans-Atlantic flight and hungry. Soon I was smiling atop a bright red double-decker bus rolling through the scenic English countryside to the bustling city of Bedford, ten miles west of RAF Chicksands and less than an hour north of London. In Bedford I settled happily into a small booth at a place called the Wimpy Bar. I had no way of knowing it, but the gregarious one-armed man who served me would become an interesting and rewarding friend.

Archie Smith was enjoying himself. The restaurant was crowded, but while the other servers were pressed for time he spoke and joked with everyone. Taking my order, he returned a few minutes later with my first Wimpy meal. Placing the wee burger in front of me, he said, "Chicksands."

Scrambling to collect my thoughts, I was unable to come up with a suitable reply.

"You're a new Yank stationed out at Chicksands," he clarified. "Welcome to the United Kingdom, mate!"

I'd never been called mate before, and I liked it. Was it my shaved head, my white socks, my American accent or the way I stared at the tiny burger that gave me away? My first British beef burger was a distant, diminutive cousin to the familiar Big Macs and Whoppers I was used to back home. It took more than a few to fill me up.

During my two-year British tour of duty I had many subsequent conversations with Archie. On one occasion we shared a couple of room-temperature ales at the Fox and Hound pub, and I asked him how he lost his arm.

He told me about growing up in Africa as the only child of Episcopal missionaries. Archie had loving parents and wonderful memories of his childhood. One afternoon the canoe he and a friend were riding in capsized. Archie was mauled by a ferocious crocodile, and his older companion was killed.

"I woke in a tent hospital. When I looked at where my left arm had been, I realized the creature had severed it at the shoulder. I turned to my right arm. Wrapped in gauze and bandages, it was immovable. Still, I was happy that I could wiggle my fingers.

"I could have been angry over the loss of my arm, or the loss of my friend, but my parents encouraged me to be thankful for my remaining limb. I took their advice, and was grateful that my life had been spared. Eventually, I recovered the use of my right arm."

That evening I also learned that Archie had once been happily married with two children, and had successfully led a large company. Highly respected and sought-after by his associates and clients, he had earned many awards, promotions and bonuses for outstanding performance. But his fame and fortune were steeped in pride. Archie's long hours, frequent travel and neglect of his family eventually led to a divorce. Soon after, he lost his job.

"Back then, life was all about me," Archie said, "I was a success in almost every aspect of my life except where it really counted. I couldn't see how much I was hurting others – especially my family. After I left the company I realized my success was superficial. A man who fails his family is not a success. I had only a few real friends. There were many calls initially and then only some. A year later there were no calls."

"Archie," I asked softly. "How do you think that shaped your understanding of the meaning of life?"

My question hit a nerve. Archie's reply was heartfelt and firm, yet at the same time his tone was forgiving. "There was no arrival. I always needed to accomplish more and more. I squandered time with my parents, with my family and with my few genuine friends. I had an insatiable need for more. Now I understand why. What we own in many ways owns us."

"I kept thinking that my success would bring happiness, but it never did. Happiness – better yet, contentment – is about learning to make do with less. It is about appreciating what you have."

Archie paused for a long minute. "Nick, the lesson, or meaning, as you put it, is this: Live a selfless balanced life without concern for your position or circumstance. Live thankfully in the present; there is no promise of tomorrow."

As a boy, Archie had loved the works of literary giants such as C.S. Lewis, G. K. Chesterton and others, and now he read nightly in a children's home run by an endearing headmaster named Sara Worthington. I had the pleasure of visiting Ms. Worthington's school on occasion to witness Archie reading. He made *The Chronicles of Narnia* come alive. It was obvious from looking into the children's eyes that they were fascinated and comforted by what he read. Those rewarding evenings listening to Archie are in great part why I had placed a priority on reading to my daughters, and to my son.

Andrew was almost asleep. When I asked him what he thought about Archie, he sleepily replied that he thought God loved Archie and spared his life so that he could make children happy by reading to them. That was my observation, too. A bloke who had mastered the eternal art of simple deeds done well, Archie daily planted saplings knowing that he would never rest in their shade. A modest man of uncommon forgiveness, thankfulness and optimism, Archie accepted responsibility for his misdeeds yet found forgiveness in his own forgiving spirit. He counted his blessings often enough to be without time for resentment or self-pity. He was an unassuming inspiration.

Reflections in a Waterfall

I frequently tramped eight or ten miles through the deepest snow to keep an appointment with a beech tree, or a yellow birch, or an old acquaintance among the pines.
- Henry David Thoreau

My friendship with Archie Smith had helped prepare me for my new role as a full-time father. I could hear Archie telling me to live positively in the present, because no one has the assurance of tomorrow. I was thinking of Archie as Andrew and I decided to begin our fifteen-month adventure together by visiting a waterfall.

With Andrew leaning on my shoulder, we perused a dog-eared book called *Waterfalls of the Southern Appalachians*. Mandy and I had used this same book early in our marriage, and I vaguely recalled scouring it with Dawn and Kimberly years ago when they were young. Andrew asked why we weren't using a newer book, and grinned broadly when I told him that I hadn't heard of anyone ever moving a waterfall.

We decided on Dukes Creek Falls near the Richard Russell Scenic Highway in Georgia. At least it was there the last time I looked. I recalled the moderate two-mile hike Mandy and I had shared a few years before. "We'll feel the spray from the gorge when we reach the observation deck," I told Andrew.

On the day of our trip in early June we were rewarded with crisp, sunny weather. Mandy made a lunch of peanut butter and banana sandwiches, apples and blueberry muffins. Driving to the Georgia Mountains Andrew took a nap, but he woke as we entered the parking area.

The downhill hike to Dukes Creek Falls was easy. Positioning ourselves on an almost-dry bench on the observation deck, we opened our lunch bags. If there was ever a more beautiful place to eat, or a tastier lunch, I'd like to find it. Surrounded by several falls with cascading whitewater plunging some two hundred feet into the turbulent gorge, it was too wonderfully noisy to talk. In comfortable silence we meditated on the multi-faceted beauty before us. Remembering the times with Dawn and Kimberly, who even today at thirty-something continue to enjoy visiting and appreciating waterfalls, I watched Andrew absorbing our special surroundings. Sharing the wonders of a waterfall, we are wealthy beyond measure.

Renewed by the light spray and by the pungent fragrance of evergreen, after an hour or so on the observation deck Andrew and I peacefully stirred from our reflections and began hiking back up the mountain to our car. I recognized with gratitude that in the simple act of sharing that quiet, reflective hour together, our father-son bond had deepened.

As we walked, Andrew peppered me with questions. I didn't know all the answers, but I tried. And maybe it is true that moving water takes longer to freeze than water in a bucket. Snakes probably are as afraid of us as we are of them. And yes, Andrew, we can almost certainly find an ice cream shop on the way home.

Routinely Spectacular

> *The tragedy of life is not so much what men suffer, but rather what they miss.*
>
> *- Thomas Carlyle*

One night Andrew asked for a new bedtime story. I told one about a time before he was born when his sisters were seven and ten. I had announced over dinner that on the next Saturday the three of us would rise before dawn.

"We'll drive over to Hallandale Beach to watch the sun rise over the Atlantic Ocean. Then we'll cross Alligator Alley to Naples and play on the beach. We'll have dinner on the beach and watch the same sun set in the Gulf," I said.

Both girls thought I was losing it. Responding virtually at the same moment, they asked, "Why?"

I explained that the idea came from a book I had recently read. The author observed that many people will get up in the wee hours of the morning to catch a glimpse of a rare comet, or they will stay up late at night to watch a lunar eclipse, but very few will make the effort to watch the everyday splendor of a sunrise or sunset. We take these daily miracles for granted.

That Saturday I roused the girls early and they wearily tumbled into the car for the ten-minute drive to the beach. On the way we stopped at a donut shop owned by my high school football coach. As the lady behind the counter placed our hot chocolate and donuts in a bag, Coach Verone emerged from the back of the shop.

"Nick!" he said, surprised to see me. "What has you up this early?"

I explained the purpose of our outing. His response, too, was a puzzled, "Why?"

Thankful that Dawn and Kimberly had chosen to slumber in the car, I wished Coach Verone good morning. As I retreated, I heard him telling the lady behind the counter for my benefit, "Good ballplayer, but obviously too many hits on the head."

At Hallandale Beach, as we sat in awe witnessing the developing morning, dark clouds moved in, enhancing the experience. The early rays of the rising sun set against the deep blue sky highlighted and energized the clouds, which waxed from gray to many shades of red and finally faded to pink. Set against this kaleidoscope of colors, the magnificent sun rose in multicolored hues of gold as we reverently observed the glory and opportunity of a new day over a rugged sea.

When it was over Dawn, my oldest daughter, assured me that the morning had been worth it. Kimberly, however, remained noncommittal and suggested that the next time we did something like this she would be content with the photographs.

We returned home and did our usual chores on an unusual morning, then began our trek across Alligator Ally. The drive included a few stops in the Florida Everglades to witness alligators, herons, egrets and other wildlife. We also visited a Seminole Indian village before checking into a motel on Florida's tranquil Gulf coast. Rather than nap, we opted to visit a nearby marina and swim in the ocean.

Sitting expectantly in our beach chairs, we again experienced the beauty of the morning. The sun that only hours before had risen triumphantly over the Atlantic now settled gracefully into the placid Gulf.

When it was over, the day had rendered our vocabularies inadequate. It was no longer necessary to answer, "Why?" Even Kimberly joined her sister Dawn in wanting to do it again one day. Watching the wondrous sunrise and sunset reaffirmed the importance of reaching out to the Creator and His creation. We longed for that someone bigger than us that the day had inspired.

Selling Sticks

Train a child in the way he should go, and when he is old he will not depart.
- Proverbs 22:6

We were attending one of the many community picnics we have with our neighbors on picturesque Berkeley Lake. Andrew wanted to climb his favorite tree, a fifteen-foot maple with many good climbing branches. I helped supervise, catching the children as they gleefully jumped from one of the lower limbs into my outstretched arms.

Later that afternoon I noticed Andrew had a partially full plastic bag of cigar-sized sticks. When I inquired as to what he was doing with them, he said that he was selling sticks. Holding up the bag so I could see the quarter and dime he had already earned, Andrew asked, "Dad, do you think they really wanted the sticks?"

I thought for a moment, then said that his customers were likely just being nice because they wanted to encourage him. Pondering my reply, Andrew asked what he could sell that people would really want.

We developed a plan. We would sell herbs and flowers grown in our family garden. We had lavender, mint, rosemary, blooming Hydrangea, Azaleas and more. Shopping around, we found Wal-Mart had the best selection of vases and dishes closest to our price point. We called the president of the Berkeley Lake Chapel to ask if we could use the chapel parking area for our venture.

Andrew and I decided that in return for the use of the parking lot we'd give the chapel forty per cent of our net proceeds. Thirty-five per cent would go into his college education fund. Andrew was excited about being able to keep the remaining twenty-five per cent to buy anything he wanted. Again and again he clarified the deal: if he did his best and held up his end of the bargain, he could buy whatever he wanted. Finally we chose the time for our sale – from 10 am to 1 pm on the Saturday before Father's Day.

Mandy agreed to help call twenty-five neighbors to make them aware of our herb and flower sale. Sidney and Gaylene Dassinger, who live across the lake, expressed regrets and said they were leaving for Nashville early that morning to visit family. They wouldn't be able to make the sale, but Sidney asked that we save something so they could buy it on their return.

We set up early under a stately old oak tree that graciously provided shade from the bright sun. Our first customers were Sidney and Gaylene Dassinger. They wouldn't admit it, but I suspected that they had delayed their departure to support an exuberant seller of sticks. Sometimes the defining moments don't come in monumental events, but in simple acts of kindness.

The first hour or so Andrew worked hard. Holding the sign Mandy had made, *Organic Herb and Flower Sale,* he waved to passers-by. Most of the people we had called showed up in the first hour, and with each sale Andrew's excitement grew. I could read his thoughts about how easy it is to sell things.

Before long we were running out of our beautiful blue Hydrangeas. Pam Williamson, another neighbor, bolstered our supply with some freshly cut Hydrangeas from her garden. I think she actually bought a couple of her own flowers! What can I say? It was another simple act of kindness.

In the first hour we sold about half our inventory. Then sales slowed. As the day grew warmer and the customers fewer, Andrew decided that he was ready to go home and that I could sell the balance of the inventory.

I told him to think again. We strategized about what we might do in the tougher market. We moved our table closer to the road for greater visibility. We decided to add verbal salutations like "good morning" and "hello" to complement our waving. We talked about positive expectations. Our neighbors had done their part. Now the work was more difficult. Now we were open to the general public.

By 1 pm our renewed efforts had paid off and we were able to return home triumphantly. Tired yet elated, we counted a total of forty-seven transactions worth $147, and a net income of $80.

The following day Andrew faithful delivered $32 to the chapel, and we wrote a check for $28 to his education savings plan. Then I handed our promising entrepreneur a crisp $20 bill, no strings attached!

On the way to Wal-Mart a concerned Andrew again sought reassurance. "Daddy, I can spend this money any way I want because I worked hard to earn it, right?"

"You got it!"

My response was well received. I followed my excited son through several isles of toys and games until finally his keen interest in trains won out. He chose a train depot for his purchase.

Some of our neighbours had felt that our Herb and Flower Sale was a lot for a four-year-old. But to us it was a microcosm of life that included the joy of family and friendships, advance preparation, cooperation and perseverance, not to mention the obvious excitement of being able to make an independent buying decision based on earning an income.

The seller of sticks had accepted responsibility and challenges. He had learned to associate work with a sense of accomplishment and wealth. Most of what we hear is soon forgotten, but what we do well often lasts a lifetime.

Chapter Three

HOME AGAIN

An almost perfect relationship with his father was the earthly root of all his wisdom. From his father, he said, he first learned that fatherhood must be at the core of the universe. He was thus prepared in an unusual way to teach that religion in which the relation of father and son is of all relations the most central.

- George MacDonald

First Things First

Juggling career and work obligations with time for family and friends often makes for a hectic life. This is why successful people prioritize. I treasure the time I've made recently for hanging out with Andrew. It has become a priority.

When we spend time together, it often includes his friends. For Andrew having fun with friends, in fact, ranks just ahead of having fun with Dad. Often on play dates I start a game, explain the basic rules, and move to the sideline. Andrew's ideal play date is when I am inconspicuously in the vicinity while he and his friends romp. I usually stay on the sidelines unless there is a sudden eerie silence, or an imminent death-defying act starting with, "Hey guys, watch this!"

Sometimes when Andrew and I ride in the car, I'll turn off the radio and use the silence for thinking. Andrew inevitably interrupts my quiet time with a comment or question. Like every child, Andrew has dozens of questions daily, and he always knows when I don't have the answer. In the past with my two girls, this syndrome led to frequent use of the encyclopedia; these days with Andrew, I rely on the internet.

Among the best indications of a father's character is the amount of time he spends with his children. I am challenged by the thought that our impressionable children are significantly yoked to us for what they are, and for what they will be. A father's commitment is a strong indicator of his child's well-being. If we are not motivated by the privilege of being a dad, we must surrender to the duty.

As fathers we may be able to ignore or deny signs of neglect in our children, but our misplaced priorities inevitably produce malignant results. The father who has unresolved issues with his own dad, and who hurts for the child within himself, is a victim. He can continue the hurtful downward cycle, or he can reverse it. In making time for his son, he reaches out to heal himself. It is in loving that we understand we are loved. When we are loved, we can find the strength to forgive. Nothing is more freeing than love and forgiveness.

Emulating this ideal may seem formidable but the stakes are high, the need is considerable, and the consequences are revolutionary. It starts with simply making time for a game of catch, and for conversation. Clearly, the question is not whether we influence our children. The question is what will our influence be?

What About That?

Until recently I worked long hours, and throughout my career I found that the best opportunity to spend time with my children was at bedtime. Mandy and I agreed that the best way to teach our son to read was to read to him early and often, and to let him observe us enjoying reading. We read to Andrew long before he spoke his first word.

Bedtime provides an opportunity to read, to share conversation and listen to music. We make significant use of the public library, and include Bible stories. One night Andrew and I read from Chick-Fil-A's free booklet *Discovering The Spirit Of America*. We talked about how America was founded by people from other countries seeking freedom, including the freedom to worship. Andrew began to understand how fortunate we are to live in a country where our basic freedoms are guaranteed. As a major train aficionado, he was also intrigued to learn about the significant role of the railroad in fulfilling the American dream of Manifest Destiny.

We also make time to listen. To show that we value Andrew's thoughts, we ask simple questions like, "What do you think about that?"

Stories are traditionally a vitally important aspect of a child's progress, and stories that honor and extol virtues are more likely to produce productive lives. Reading Ralph Waldo Emerson one night, I came across this line: "The creation of a thousand forests is in one acorn."

"What do you think about that?" I asked Andrew.

"Must of been a 'normous corn," he replied.

Brahms, Bach and Beethoven

Music of the great composers sends the devil packing. In music, we are inspired to express our most meaningful feelings.

- author unknown

My friend Les Hewitt, an international performance coach and best-selling co-author of *The Power of Focus,* taught me about the benefits of Baroque music. The prevailing style of classical composition and performance from the end of the sixteenth century to the beginning of the eighteenth century, Baroque music is conducive to the learning process. Some of the more prominent compositions of this period were written by Bach, Vivaldi and Handel.

Andrew is also fond of classical music, including Baroque compositions, and has listened to Mozart for Kids from an early age. We often listen to classical music in the background when meditating and reading. Some nights we make the great compositions a bedtime feature, and some nights our bedtime routine includes a sing-along. We print lyrics off the internet and crank up favorites like *Take It Easy, My Girl* and *Peaceful Easy Feeling,* enthusiastically singing along with the Eagles and the Temptations.

One of our favorite bedtime books is *Spiritual Moments with the Great Composers* by Patrick Kavanaugh. Reading this book, we learned that Ludwig van Beethoven wrote his masterpiece, *Symphony No. 9,* during one of the more difficult times of his relatively short life. Incredibly, Beethoven was hearing-impaired. Yet his life and works provide strong testimony to accomplishment despite difficulties – difficulties that invariably accompany every life.

Happy Endings

What do Helen Keller, Martin Luther King Jr., Lance Armstrong and Ronald Reagan have in common?
The lives of a blind author, black pastor, superb athlete and elder statesmen were challenged, but they gave us many happy endings. In confronting physical disabilities, bigotry, disease and tyranny, these outstanding individuals inspire us to stretch higher in our own beliefs.

In early childhood Helen Keller lost her sight and hearing to illness. A devoted friendship with her teacher, Anne Sullivan, provided the opportunity to learn and to communicate in an extraordinary manner. Sullivan taught her charge to speak by touching the lips and throats of others, and by finger-spelling letters on the palm of their hands. Later Keller learned Braille and began to read – not only in English, but also in French, German, Greek and Latin. Eventually she wrote two books and acted in a movie. Helen Keller's determination and persistence saw her through college with honors. Despite the formidable obstacles of blindness and deafness, she dedicated her life to the betterment of others, especially the blind and hearing-impaired. Helen Keller's faith, optimism, and achievements beg this question: What excuse do I have for not succeeding in God's purpose for my life?

In his *Letter from a Birmingham Jail*, Martin Luther King Jr. wrote of the need for non-violent civil disobedience to accomplish the goal of equality for blacks in America. Dr. King was criticized by whites and blacks alike for his determined actions. In response, he quoted Saint Augustine. "An unjust law is no law at all."

"One who breaks an unjust law must do it openly, lovingly... and with a willingness to accept the penalty," Dr. King wrote. Great achievement is often preceded by criticism and adversity. The persistence of Dr. Martin Luther King Jr. resulted in a significant human rights milestone and landmark legislation – the Civil Rights Act of 1964.

The Tour de France bicycle race is one of the most formidable of all sporting events, and testicular cancer is one of the most deadly of all cancers. Yet testicular cancer survivor Lance Armstrong is an unprecedented seven time champion of the Tour de France. A role model for his unyielding optimism and determination, Armstrong inspires us to be our best.

As president of the United States, Ronald Reagan faced tragedy with courage and humor. In March 1981 he had just spoken to 3,500 members of the AFL-CIO in Washington, DC when he and several others were shot in a mindless act. The bullet that hit President Reagan came within an inch of hitting his heart. Coughing up blood and hardly breathing, he walked into the hospital before finally collapsing.

When the First Lady arrived at his side he said, "Honey, I forgot to duck."

Shortly before being sedated for three hours of life-saving surgery, the president looked at the surgeons and quipped, "I hope you're Republicans."

"Today, Mr. President, we're all Republicans," one of the doctors replied.

Heroes have that affect on people. Accomplishment is often accompanied by adversity but even in adversity, or perhaps especially in adversity, those who make a difference in the world rise above themselves. Helen Keller, Martin Luther King, Lance Armstrong and Ronald Reagan were selfless heroes who rose above adversity. They shared qualities that I almost reluctantly wish for my own son. I say almost reluctantly because great achievement is almost always accompanied by great adversity.

Fun In East Newnan

"A good scare is in many ways like good advice."

- Anon

Andrew is intrigued by accounts of my childhood, so we decided to spend a day together in East Newnan, Georgia. I grew up in Miami, but was born in Newnan and spent every summer of my young life at the home of my wonderful maternal grandparents,

Robert and Minnie Watson.

Our day trip to East Newnan officially began when we exited the hectic interstate at historic College Park. The more interesting Highway 29 closely parallels storied old towns and busy railway lines. Driving through seasoned cities like Fairburn, we came upon several freight trains. I was pleased to see Andrew excitedly exchanging waves with the engineers.

My observation of train engineers is that they are free spirits piloting vestiges of Americana across our country. Ambassadors of a bygone era rumbling through cities and towns with horns blasting and whistles blowing, never missing the opportunity to wave, they are heroes to our children. It was gratifying to witness so much enthusiasm from my four-year-old.

When we reached our destination we drove to the East Newnan Mill, where my granddad, Robert Watson, worked for most of his career. We parked the car and walked to a nearby beaver pond. When I was eight I had fallen into that pond and been fished out by an older boy. Andrew wanted to see the exact place where I had tumbled into the water.
From there we followed the stream into the woods. It was not much different than when I was a boy. The short hike brought back fond memories, some of which I shared with Andrew as we sat beside the brook for a calming spell. He was especially intrigued by a story about Ricky Cheeves and me escaping from dangerous hobos.

In the days of my youth the railroad tracks had provided a shortcut to the Newnan town square. At age nine or ten Ricky and I had been walking along the tracks back to East Newnan from the Montgomery Ward store in Newnan's town square, where that morning I'd purchased a snappy pair of Pat Boone white bucks. For some reason I decided to wear the white bucks home. Placing my old shoes in the Montgomery Ward shopping bag,

Ricky and I began walking the rails.

About halfway between town and the East Newnan Mill we approached a tattered trackside encampment. Two scruffy men appeared and summoned Ricky and me. Unkempt and gruff, they asked what I had in my shopping bag. The larger man demanded the bag, and the smaller man wanted my new white bucks.

Ricky and I exchanged quick, incredulous glances. Like Tom Sawyer and Huck Finn before us, we spun around and started running. Peppering us with ripe expletives the hostile hobos maintained hot pursuit, but they soon lost ground to our frantic pace. We scrambled along the railroad ties to the mill, and were never so glad to see the busy workers.

The fear that pulsed through our veins didn't dampen the delight of our triumphant escape, but Ricky and I decided it would be best to keep the chance encounter with the hobos just between us. Reluctantly I discarded my new shoes, now covered with railroad tar. They would elicit questions I didn't want to answer – especially the question I couldn't answer: "Why in the world did you wear your white bucks out the Montgomery Ward door?"

Andrew and I returned to our car and drove a mile or so to the former home of my grandparents. The small walking bridge connecting their property to the village road was of most interest to Andrew. I had told him about how my siblings, cousins and I had used the area under the small bridge as our clubhouse. The Watson grandchildren often hid under the bridge to greet our granddad on his return from the mill. The lanky, loving man always managed to have a warm smile and bag of highly prized corn chips for us. Listening to my stories, Andrew intently climbed under the bridge to share the experience of hiding there.

Crossing the small bridge, fond memories of the times we had in, around and under the old house at 40 Haynes Street came back to me. I continued to narrate stories to my fascinated son.

"There were no banks in East Newnan village, so any money I earned from chores like cutting grass, drying dishes and picking produce went straight into my bright-red Prince Albert tobacco tin. I had a special place under the house to hide the canister. It stayed there until I'd saved enough for a Saturday morning at the Alamo Theatre."

"My granddad worked hard all his life, but he died having accumulated little in material wealth. However, he was respected by everyone who knew him. We always felt his love, and the love of our grandmother. They both made time for us in many ways. I don't recall either of them spending much money on entertainment or gifts, but we felt that we had plenty. We had no TV, but there was always so much to do.

I told Andrew about walking with my granddad to the top of the hill where there was an abandoned schoolhouse. Every child in Newnan knew that the schoolhouse was haunted. We also hiked to the Beaver Branch blackberry patch, where an afternoon of berry picking would net us enough berries for one of grandmother's large, savory cobblers. We helped in the garden, played hide and seek and rode handmade stick horses. We built go-carts with leftover wood, a handful of nails and an old door spring. By day we sailed out over the banister on the front-porch swing, and at night we sat serenely listening to the adults talk, gazing at a million stars and waiting for the watermelon behind the front door to be cut. We had little in the way of things, but we were rich.

A man is wealthy in proportion to the things he can do without.

- Epicurus

Too often we rob our children of the satisfaction of earning something. For many families, and for many children, the issue is having too much.

Many of today's children are conditioned to expect more. In spite of all they have, they are unfulfilled and seemingly have no point of satisfaction. Bedrooms, playrooms, garages, and yards are littered with toys, games and other things. For many, too much is not enough. Never before have children been given so much where so little is required and so little is appreciated.

> *Mere wealth can't bring us happiness,*
> *Mere wealth can't make us glad.*
> *But we'll always take a shot, I guess,*
> *At being rich and sad.*
> *- C.C. Colton*

Andrew and I crossed what had been a dirt road when I was a child but was now paved. Directly in front of my grandparents' former home was the well-manicured home of the Rollins family. Jake and Lois Rollins had two beautiful daughters about the same age as my brothers and I. We often played together in the summers of long ago, the summers of Elvis, poodle skirts and drive-in movies.

Jake Rollins had passed away, the girls were grown with families, and Lois now lived alone. A spry eighty-something, she was still working in the same well-tended flower garden as Andrew and I approached her.

"Lois, do you know who I am?" I asked, pointing at my son. "People say I looked like him when I was his age."

Intently studying both of us, a smile grew on her still-beautiful face. "Why, you're little Nicky!"

We laughed and chatted for a while, catching up on news about her daughters and the neighbors. Out of the corner of my eye I watched Andrew, who was obviously fascinated by this display of the enduring and priceless value of friendships. As we bid Lois farewell with a hug, she gave us directions to the home of another old friend.

The last time I had visited Morgan Couch, Dwight Eisenhower was president. I'd lost track of him over the years, but we'd mend that today. Morgan and I had been industrious boys who partnered to cut grass and weeds around the village using only a sling blade. It was hard work, but it always culminated in a trip to Jay's General Store. At the store Morgan's favorite snack was a Banana Moon Pie and a cool Nehi grape soda. Holding the frosty soda was soothing to young hands blistered by hours of slinging.

The reunion with Morgan was also rewarding as we laughingly recalled our childhood adventures. A corroborating witness, Morgan validated many of the stories I'd shared with Andrew, including another of his favorites, the one about my scary after-dark visit to the old schoolhouse.

Andrew's grandmother, my mom, had attended school in that building, but for many years it had sat on top of the hill, abandoned except for what was widely believed among the local children to be a resident ghost. One frightening night I had gone in alone to impress Morgan, Ricky and Harold, who watched from a safe distance believing I was unlikely to return. Inside the schoolhouse a dusty piano was covered with cobwebs. Sitting under the piano in the dark, terrified, I remained motionless, measuring every breath, reluctantly willing the ghost to appear. The darkness intensified and magnified every sound. I was sure the creature haunting the place would hear my racing heart!

Laughing at the memory, Morgan confirmed my story as Andrew looked up at me with newfound respect.

"Do you think the ghost might still be in the area?" he asked.

We went to find out, even though Morgan reminded us that the schoolhouse had been reduced to ashes many years before. Andrew wondered if the ghost had been playing with matches.

The road leading to the schoolhouse was overgrown, so we walked up the hill. After forty minutes scouring the brush, brambles and trees for what might be left of the building, we decided to rest and rethink our search.

"I really enjoyed playing detective when I was a kid," I told Andrew. "Today, let's be detectives."

Andrew agreed that we were solving a mystery, and that it was fun. His buddy, Scooby Doo, would be proud. Our time for thought resulted in two important clues. If the schoolhouse had burnt to the ground twenty years before, we would be looking for a cluster of small trees. As well, the entrance had featured a staircase made of concrete covered with pea rock, the same material as the walking bridge that led to the home of my grandparents. The staircase would not have been consumed by the fire.

With new life infused in our search, we focused on finding the staircase. Before long we discovered a clump of smaller trees. Approaching the trees, we saw the staircase! Excitedly we climbed to the top. Sitting together, Andrew confirmed that these were the very same stairs his frightened father had traversed to impress his friends one dark and scary night.

Looking out over the former school grounds, the afternoon sun filtered through an impressive, hundred-year-old oak tree. I told Andrew that this same tree had offered me shade in the summer of 1953 during one of my most rewarding childhood jobs. Harold Yarborough and I had cleaned bricks of their mortar for a penny each. Each week of diligent work had culminated in a pile of clean bricks and more than enough cash to meet a small boy's needs.

Some of my brick money each week was deposited in my bright-red Prince Albert tobacco tin. I was saving for a Daisy BB gun and for a Red Flyer wagon. The rest was reserved for Saturday movies. Sitting in the darkened theater with warm popcorn and a cold Coke, Harold and I admiringly rode with Roy Rogers and Dale Evans as they rounded up scoundrels. We also watched Peter Pan and shared his desire to never grow up.

Andrew and I walked over to the ancient oak to look for a brick, perhaps one that I had cleaned a half-century before. Incredibly, to our great delight we found a brick buried in the undergrowth. We unearthed our treasure and brought it home. The chunk of clay now holds a position of honor in our family awards case. It reminds us of the joy of friendship and work. It reminds us to live every day with anticipation and appreciation.

Other interesting stops before we left Newnan included the remains of Jay's General Store and the waterworks where picnics always featured my grandmother's prized fried chicken along with real lemonade and pesky yellow jackets. Have you ever been stung by a yellow jacket? If you can't remember, you've never been stung by a yellow jacket.

It was almost dark when we reached the interstate. We were returning home pleasantly spent from our all-day outing. I tilted the rearview mirror and found comfort in the sight of my son's sleepy face. Seeing me gazing lovingly at him in the mirror, Andrew said, "Daddy, I want us to move to Newnan."

Chapter Four

A WORLD VIEW

*There is just one way to train up a child in the way he should
go and that is to travel that way yourself.*

- Abraham Lincoln

Surely four is too young for a child to have a world view, but even
as toddlers our children start forming opinions about what they
believe and value. Much of what they believe comes from us. As
parents, what we believe and what we do has a lasting influence
on the lives of our children.

Occasionally I recall the advice my dad gave me, but more often
I find myself doing the same things he did. I don't think it is co-
incidental that many of my dad's habits have become my own. I
am thankful for the many good habits I observed – habits that
arose from his love for his family, and from his strong work ethic.

Dad also did things he didn't want me to embrace. He wanted his
children to be better and to do better than he had. He encouraged
us to emulate the good and to spurn the faults. This was good
advice, and we can all learn from it. We can choose to embrace

the good and to spurn the faults. It is incumbent on every child, and on every father, to break the cycle of faults. It takes courage to change but replacing faulty actions, such as frequently missing family dinners, with good habits will change generations of lives.

Children who regularly eat dinner with their parents are healthier, both physically and emotionally, than children who do not. This seems basic and obvious to me now, but it wasn't always as clear. Before I established my new priorities about what was most important to me– my faith, my family and my health – there were many times in my career when I felt that I just couldn't make it home for dinner.

Families who are close understand that dinner is about more than eating. It is about togetherness. Being home for dinner is a commitment. Somewhere down the line, that commitment will earn us a place setting at the dinner table of our children.

Andy's Trout Farm

It is better to practice it than to know how to define it.

- Thomas a Kempis

One weekend Mandy, Andrew and I journeyed to Andy's Trout Farm and Cabins, a rustic mountain retreat on Betty's Creek Road near the border of Georgia and North Carolina. Like Andy, the trout farm is comfortably laid-back and neighborly. Going there is like traveling back to a simpler time of trout fishing with worms and a cane pole, of hiking through woods redolent with an abundance of healing fragrances.

Many of the pastoral cabins are located right on Betty's Creek. Sitting on the covered front porch of our rented cabin, we were treated to the wonderful sounds of purposeful white water. It was a perfect evening for a modest dinner, bedtime story and restful sleep. As we sat enjoying the aural treat of rushing water, a steady rain began falling. Soon thunder and lighting began illuminating the gray Carolina heavens. With the first clap of thunder Mandy, who is cautious about stormy weather, retreated into the tiny cabin while Andrew and I remained on the front porch only a few feet away from the rising creek.

It was a grand storm, inspiring and exhilarating. We sat watching tumultuous Betty's Creek rushing past, enjoying the feeling of being scarcely out of the weather. The storm continued long into the night. With no clock, radio or television in the cabin I don't know when we turned in, but we sure slept soundly.

The next morning the rain was gone. Mandy prepared cereal and bananas for breakfast then drove into the nearby town of Dillard to do a little shopping while Andrew and I set out for a hike in the woods. We followed a path through the forest until we came to a meadow, then we walked alongside a creek that led to the waterfall that was the source of Andy's trout ponds. Dangling our bare feet in the chilly creek, Andrew asked for a story.

"When I was a boy," I began, "Granddad Watson would take us for walks in the woods. Granddad was concerned that the family dog, Rex, would get hurt in the briar patches. We were always disappointed when he would instruct Rex to stay home. But Rex had his tricks and sure enough, the beagle would always plead his way into the soft spot in granddad's heart. Soon Rex would be part of the happy, rag-tag bunch of youngsters walking and running to keep pace with granddad."

My story was interrupted when three large deer sprinted past. Removing our feet from the cold water, we decided to follow the creek back downstream to a narrowing where we could cross. From the safety of our cabin porch, Andrew asked if the deer rushing past had scared me. I told him the deer hadn't frightened me, but I did wonder what had spooked them.

Mandy was already at the cabin with lunch prepared. Sharing

the meal, we sat on the porch and talked. That evening, we decided, we'd have fresh trout for dinner. Andrew's excitement grew as our host gathered a cane pole, some worms and a bucket for our catch. Directing us to the appropriate pond, Andy's parting comment was the same as it had been thirty years before when I had been here with Dawn and Kimberly.

"Please don't throw any back."

An Infinite Connection

Andrew caught the limit of trout dictated by Dad's budget in a little over an hour. Andy cleaned the five fish and when he offered our son the opportunity to help, Andrew became his apprentice, guts and all.

Back at our cabin with our catch on ice, we decided to visit historic Dillard House where presidents and corporate tycoons of a bygone era had lodged and dined. Starting at the Dillard House petting zoo, Andrew fed and patted a variety of farm animals. He quickly learned to keep his palm flat when feeding the horses and goats – I advised him to count his fingers after a goat nipped at them.

Dillard House is surrounded by expansive fields of vegetables. A mountain range just beyond the fields is a source of water for the Tennessee River, and the river is a source of irrigation for the produce. Much as I had done in my own childhood, we delighted in skipping rocks across the river. Returning to the Dillard House complex we noticed a makeshift sign on one of the buildings: "Our dinner vegetables were in the field this morning."

That evening on the porch of our comfortable old cabin the three of us shared a delicious dinner of trout and fresh Dillard House vegetables. For dessert we enjoyed a handful of vanilla wafers, a cup of hot cocoa and a captivating, star-filled sky.

After dinner we built a campfire in front of the cabin and watched the creek flowing by. Gazing up at the brilliant heavens, lulled by the flames into a state of relaxed peacefulness, we understood that we were witnessing the incomprehensible. Experiencing tranquility beyond our understanding, we felt infinitely connected.

Five Words or Less

The next morning we left Andy's Trout Farm and Cabins. Journeying further north and east, we came to the quaint town of Dillsboro, North Carolina. Dillsboro is home of the Great Smokey Mountain Railroad. We secured tickets for a four-hour round-trip excursion to Bryson City.

With a seasoned diesel pulling the historic, restored passenger cars, our route took us through mature forest paralleling the scenic Tuckasegee River. We passed picturesque farms, intriguing towns and numerous points of interest including the dark Cowee Tunnel.

After sharing a pizza lunch in Bryson City, Mandy went exploring in town while Andrew and I checked out river rafting trips for a future date. We found a playground where Andrew easily made friends while I sat on a bench beside a man name Stu. Stu was politely humored when I explained that my son is my grandchildren's uncle. He was further amused when Andrew readily complied with two simple requests I made.

"Don't jump from there!" I said, bringing a quick halt to one of Andrew's potentially death-defying acts.

"I think you should apologize," I said on the second occasion, when Andrew and another child accidentally collided while playing tag.

"How do you do that?" Stu asked, impressed by Andrew's quick response and by our father-son rapport.

My simple and straightforward answer was that early on in Andrew's life I had decided that mutual respect would make our relationship much better. Mutual respect is the basis for my using the five-words-or-less rule. Polite imperatives such as "let's eat," "don't do that," and "it's time for bed," are better than confusing, vague suggestions.

I also told Stu that I often gave Andrew some lead time in advance of an imminent departure. "We need to leave in fifteen minutes," gives him time to wind down and to feel somewhat in control.

I want Andrew to be thankful for all that he has, not always pining for more. Too often we whine about what we don't have, instead of being grateful for what we do have. I think it starts on the playground.

That's why I also let him respectfully appeal my decision by asking to stay a little while longer. I often agree, but Andrew knows that if I say no, I still want a smile for the good time he has already had.

One weekend Andrew demonstrated that he was growing in the gift of being thankful. We took Mandy's Volvo on a kayak river trip, but after unloading the kayaks at the river we couldn't raise the electric passenger-side window. There was a forecast of rain for the following day so that night Andrew and I included the window in our prayer. The next morning we started the Volvo and again attempted to close the window. It rose three-quarters of the way, but stopped. It was easier to protect the car's interior with a plastic garden bag after the window rose most of the way, but I wanted Andrew's take on why it hadn't closed all of the way.

"What's the deal with God?" I asked Andrew.

"I think He wanted to see if we would be thankful for how high it went, or upset that it didn't go up all the way."

Stu and I continued talking on the bench. "Ten more minutes," I called to Andrew.

About ten minutes later Stu and I parted company with a handshake and a smile. As we left, Stu told me he was going to give my five-words-or-less rule, lead time and respectful appeal methods a try.

Wild at Heart

One day I received a phone call from Ken Cox, a former business associate and friend. He had just finished reading a best-seller by John Eldredge that he thought I'd enjoy. At Ken's prompting, I purchased *Wild at Heart, Discovering the Secret of a Man's Soul*. I read the book in one evening, and later re-read it.

In Wild at Heart, John Eldredge invites men to recover their masculine heart, defined in the image of a passionate God. And he invites women to discover the secret of a man's soul and to delight in the strength and wildness men were created to offer. (Thomas Nelson Publishers)

Soon after I read *Wild at Heart* my son corrected something I said while he was helping Mandy and I straighten up the house. "Andrew, you are such a nice boy," I said.

"Daddy, I'm not a nice boy. I'm a pirate!" was Andrew's prompt and determined response.

I am most thankful to be living with a pirate. He has manners, but being well-mannered is not his primary focus. Andrew is led by a bold and courageous heart. He bathes and brushes his teeth, but he is none-the-less a free spirit with a strong attachment to swords, gold coins and the Jolly Roger that flies prominently from our canoe.

One afternoon as the pirate and I were canoeing around our lake a neighbor's daughter, Manning, who is a year older than Andrew, summoned us from the shore of her family's home. We paddled over to greet her.

"I want you to know Andrew was naughty," she said. Hmm, I thought, this is coming earlier than anticipated, even for a buccaneer.

An articulate five-year-old, Manning explained that at our last community picnic Andrew had ascended to the top of the children's favorite climbing tree but had refused to give up his lofty perch to her, or to anyone else. I took deft glances at my son, who was listening intently as Manning finished her story. Andrew knows we hold him accountable for his actions, but he seemed undisturbed by the portrayal.

"Manning, I'm sorry you weren't able to spend more time on top of the maple tree, but Andrew is not a nice boy. He's a pirate," I replied.

Dismissing my comment, Manning assured us that her mother would hear about my response. As we pushed away from shore I thought, "That's the kind of gal I want Andrew to marry – bright and beautiful, with a strong sense of adventure and accountability." However, Manning apparently rethought the situation. A conversation I happened to have with her mom, Kathy, a week or so later indicated that Manning hadn't turned us in.

I knew I had done the right thing in supporting my son. When we resumed paddling, Andrew turned to look at me.

"What she told you, Dad, it was true."

"Good, son," I said with a smile that I trusted would communicate my joy at being the father of a pirate. "Nothing worthwhile ever comes easy, but remember that sharing what we have makes it worth having."

One Man's Treasure

Mandy suggested that Andrew and I visit the Lanier Museum on one of our day trips. We gathered information on the internet and began planning our trip. The most appealing information was that the museum was populated with live venomous and non-venomous snakes.

It was a beautiful day for a drive. On the southern border of Lake Lanier we were welcomed to the museum by a knowledgeable young ranger who quickly allayed Andrew's concern about the potential of Berkeley Lake, where we live, having the aggressive and poisonous Cottonmouth snake, also known as the Water Moccasin.

This was contrary to an eccentric older neighbor's warnings about regular sightings of the reptile in our lake. Our guide assured us that Water Moccasins need the warmer weather of South Georgia and Florida. This was another reason for us to like winter. We know the Cottonmouth has an important role in the ecology and we like snakes, but we prefer not to swim with the venomous ones.

Andrew's eyes went back and forth from the guide to the snakes as she spoke about the various serpents. We walked attentively from cage to aquarium gathering interesting facts about Copperheads, Water Snakes, Black Snakes and Rat Snakes. But it was the Ring Snake the guide placed in his hands that brought the biggest smile to Andrew's face.

It was a rewarding tour, and it gave Andrew a better appreciation for the value of snakes in the ecology. Most of the fear we carried into the museum was replaced by a keener interest in serpents. As we drove home, Andrew asked for a story.

After facing down so many snake-related fears, I thought it appropriate to talk about courage. I focused on the courage of a man called Gordo, an astronaut who showed great courage in his calling. I told Andrew that the story came from Tom Wolfe's best-selling book, *The Right Stuff.*

Gordon Cooper prepared for his opportunity to enter outer space. He understood his mission and approached his perilous role with confidence. Here's how Tom Wolfe told it:

Early in the morning of May 15, (1963) while it was still dark, Gordo was inserted into the little human holster atop the rocket. As usual there was a long hold before the lift-off. The doctors monitoring the biomedical telemetry began noticing something very odd. In fact, they couldn't believe it. Every objective reading of the calibrations and printouts indicated......the astronaut had gone to sleep! The man was up there stacking Z's on top of a rocket loaded with 200,000 pounds of liquid oxygen!

- Tom Wolfe

As we neared home I told Andrew we'd go by the bank to place a savings bond in our deposit box. His eyes lit up when I told him we had a pirate's bounty of silver and gold stowed in the box. When I asked if he wanted to see the loot, I received an enthusiastic, "Yes!"

The teller escorted us to a private room. With Andrew expectantly looking on, I opened the lid and retrieved a few one-ounce silver coins, then reached in and withdrew two gold coins. Holding the gold American Eagles in hands barely the size of the coins, Andrew excitedly inquired, "Do they have chocolate in them?"

First Class on the Wrong Plane

The major advances in civilization are processes which all but wreck the societies in which they occur.
                    - Alfred North Whitehead

I don't buy into what some call chronological evolution – the belief that all things improve over time. That is, what we are and have today is better than what we were or had in the past. While I understand that some things have improved over time, I also know that some things have not. What is new is not necessarily better than what is old. Much of what we had in the past is superior to what we have today. Just because we have more, and we do more things faster, doesn't mean that we've progressed.

What's not better now?

Once-promising television has evolved into a mind-numbing wasteland crowded with commercials and bad programming, and movies are even worse, if that's possible. What if the next Academy Awards vanity parade was cancelled? What if the money spent on tuxedos, designer dresses and jewelry was instead used to fund a charity? What if advertisers also contributed the many thousands of dollars they earmark for the awards program? We could feed the destitute of a small nation. That would be progress.

What else is not better?

Far too many people no longer treat dinner as a special time to be home with family sharing nutritious food and conversation. We eat out more than ever, and often alone. Our diets are the worst they have ever been. We are a nation that has found it necessary to add "grossly obese" to our weight categories.

This year more Americans will be diagnosed with heart disease, cancer and diabetes than ever before. Moreover, those needing help for psychological distress founded in loneliness grows annually, and tragically this includes an increasing number of children.

Time-saving gadgets like cell phones, Blackberries and email further isolate us from family and friends. We are saving time so we can work longer. In our pride we are accessible to everyone except family and friends. We're getting ahead, but we're not quite sure where we're going.

 I read where a man lost his keys at the airport and had to take a cab home. When he knocked on the front door and his five-year-old son answered, the child turned and yelled, "Mommy, there's a man at the door."

What was better back then?

We were happier and healthier when neighbors sat on front porches to visit, when families made time to eat dinner together, when kids returned from school to find a parent at home, when bedtime stories were a tradition and when Willie Mays was our favorite celebrity.

We are killing ourselves working to be in control – yet we are only a phone call, or a test result – away from losing control. We are accumulating so much so that one day we will finally have it all, yet too many of us arrive alone. Someone asked how much mega-wealthy J.D. Rockefeller left behind when he died. The response, of course, is, "All of it."

Where have you gone, Joe DiMaggio?

Chapter Five

ON TOP OF THE WORLD

Examine yourself; discover where your true chance of greatness lies. Seize that chance and let no power or persuasion deter you from your task.

- Schoolmaster in Chariots of Fire

We encourage Andrew to understand that God made him uniquely special. He has been given talents so he may discover them, hone them and lead a fruitful life. This is true for all children.

Every child, whether poor or born into wealth and privilege, can make a meaningful contribution. Monumental things still need to be done in the world, and discovering solutions for famine and disease are not the least of them. But achieving feats of this nature is likely for only a relatively few individuals, while simple things like offering a hand and a smile can be performed by everyone. Smiling has no language barrier. Smiling faces are always beautiful, and they usually set off a wave of goodwill.

Mother Teresa, who led a life of simple things done well, once said, "Every time you smile at someone it is an action of love, a gift to that person, a beautiful thing. A somewhat devious friend told me that he smiled often because he liked having people wonder what he was up to. Whatever the reason, this simple act has life-changing potential, both for the giver and for the receiver.

Hotel Heaven

What is a success?
To laugh often and much;
To win the respect of intelligent people and the affection of children;
To earn the appreciation of honest critics and endure the betrayal of false friends;
To appreciate beauty;
To find the best in others;
To leave the world a bit better, whether by a healthy child, a garden patch or a redeemed social condition;
To know even one life has breathed easier because you have lived;
That is to have succeeded.

- Ralph Waldo Emerson

One day Andrew and I drove to the nearby Metropolitan Atlanta Rapid Transit Authority (MARTA) station and took a commuter train into Atlanta. With Andrew sitting on my lap, we gazed out at freight trains and cemeteries, at the city of Chamblee, at graffiti and lush, green kudzu, at the MARTA terminal near Atlantic Station, and then finally at our destination, bustling downtown Atlanta.

Rising up from the depths of the station on one of the world's steepest escalators, we ascended to the Peachtree Center and walked a short distance to the Westin Peachtree Plaza. When it opened in 1976, the Peachtree Plaza was the world's tallest hotel. Cast in reflective glass with a cylindrical shape towering an impressive eighty-two stories above ground, the building dwarfs all others around it. Inside, a small cylinder ascending the full height of the hotel accommodates two glass elevators.

The uppermost floors hold the Sun Dial Restaurant, a revolving restaurant offering panoramic views of the city.

Andrew knew that I had often stayed at the Peachtree Plaza when I lived in Ft. Lauderdale and came to Atlanta for business. Looking up at the imposing glass elevator, he was noticeably apprehensive. Inside, rising higher and higher, he said in a small voice, "Daddy, let's take the stairs when we go down."

From the top, our panoramic view was stunning. Andrew's initial fear soon faded as he scampered around observing the bird's-eye view of landmarks such as Georgia Institute of Technology, Coca Cola international headquarters, Stone Mountain and the world's busiest airport. Far below was the blue-domed roof of the Hyatt Regency Hotel. Andrew was amused to hear that the twenty-two-story Hyatt had for a time been Atlanta's tallest hotel.

His fear completely gone, after enjoying a beverage in the revolving Sun Dial restaurant Andrew didn't want to leave our lofty perch. When we did depart, he insisted on taking the glass elevator down. Pressing his nose to the glass, he craned his neck for a better view.

I wasn't quite as confident. With one sweaty palm holding the handrail and the other tightly gripping Andrew's hand, I admonished my son not to stand so close to the glass. Arriving back at the lobby my relief must have been evident, because a lady who shared our ride remarked on the different countenances of father and son.

"I admire your son's courage," she said, "but I'm with you. That was scary."

Sharing a nervous laugh, we agreed that descending was less menacing than ascending – if anything went wrong, we'd already be heading in the right direction.

From the Westin, Andrew and I made our way to the Marriott Marquis Hotel using the protected passageway connecting Atlanta's convention hotels. The Marquis is not as tall as the Westin, but it is nonetheless an impressive building. The view from the glass elevator in the Marquis is not out over the city, but into the cavernous luxury of its lobby. Looking down, we saw the lobby café and decided to share a snack there.

The Westin Peachtree Plaza may not be Mt. Everest, and Andrew and I are not Sir Edmund Percival Hillary and Tenzing Norgay reaching the summit in 1953. But don't tell that to my intrepid son. He was on top of the world that day.

Leaving the Marriott with a sense of accomplishment and a spring in our step, we continued our journey toward Piedmont Park. Outside Morton's Steakhouse, we came upon some fountains. It was a hot afternoon and we found the cooling spray most refreshing. Suddenly, without notice, Andrew darted into the fountains. He returned with a big smile on his face and his clothes soaking wet.

"Daddy, that was great!"

Mandy wisely encourages me to pack a change of clothes on our day jaunts, but I hadn't this time. Returning to the Marriott, we found a kindhearted chambermaid who laughingly offered the use of a towel and a bathroom. Andrew removed his drenched clothing and I rang out most of the water. Dressing in his damp clothes, he wasn't pleased.

We thanked the amused chambermaid and asked that she give our regards to Mr. Marriott, setting off more peals of laughter. In Piedmont Park we sat in the shade of a group of stately oaks observing the beautiful, growing Atlanta skyline and enjoying the sweet aroma of jasmine on summer breezes. It was renewing and calming to be outdoors. Andrew laughed as I retold a story

about one of Mandy's friends, a lady who so dislikes being outdoors that she won't even lower the window on her car.

When he asked for a riddle, I told him this one. "There are two
men. One believes in miracles, and the other does not believe in
miracles. Which man is right?"

Having heard this riddle before, Andrew answered confidently.
"They are both right."

Indeed. You either believe in the supernatural act of a miracle,
or you rationalize the act by giving credit to someone, or something, other than God.

One day sitting on a park bench near home, I had a conversation
with a kindly man whose Downs Syndrome daughter was playing nearby. His daughter told me she was going to be a nurse.
Seeing the smile that broke across my face, she inquired, "Do
you think I will be a good nurse?"

"Absolutely! I think you will be a very good nurse," I affirmed.

"Yes! Yes! Yes!" she exclaimed in pleasure, hopping around
excitedly.

I couldn't read her quiet father, but a couple of weeks later I saw
the man in the grocery store by himself. Seeking him out, I said,
"I apologize if I offended you that day in the park."

He admitted that he initially thought I had offered his daughter
false hope, but had since decided there was no harm done. He
thanked me for showing an interest in his daughter, and we departed with a handshake.

The challenge of being a good parent is to lead by example, but it
is also gratifying when we see our children surpassing our own

station in life. To my mind, the Downs Syndrome girl's hope is not false. Her father was resigned to reality, but miracles go beyond reality. With each passing year, science finds new cures. What a parent tells a child has a significant influence on what that child believes he or she can do.

A parent who tells a child that she is special and that God has a plan for her life is absolutely right. A parent who tells a child that she will not amount to much is unfortunately also often right. Tragically, many prisoners had parents who told them they were no good and that one day they would end up in prison.

If the parent does not believe in the child, who will? We help our children reach their full potential when we encourage them to appreciate what others have accomplished, and the obstacles they had to overcome.

Gazing from a rooftop or mountaintop, a child comes to appreciate how much more there is beyond the ordinary. Parents too often temper the dreams of children by attempting to protect them from the pain of failure, or to spare them disappointment. When we ourselves are fearful of leaving the pack, we discourage those around us to seek to be different, and to seek to make a difference. We act as if success can come without failure.

Mountains become narrower at the summit for a reason – unfortunately, there is no need for more room as fewer people make the attempt to go there.

Helen Keller had strong faith, and she expected God's involvement in her life. Because she believed, her life was in many ways a miracle. Keller was the first deaf and blind person to graduate college. She became a prolific best-selling author and crusader of many worthy causes including women's suffrage.

Miracles still happen for those who believe.

Every Day's a Good Day

What may be done at any time will be done at no time.

- Scottish proverb

Soon after we had enjoyed the top of Georgia's tallest hotel, it seemed fitting that we would visit Georgia's highest mountain. Over breakfast I asked Andrew if he'd like to go to Brasstown Bald.

Later in the day we made plans over dinner and Mandy commented on our spontaneity. Andrew wanted to know the definition of spontaneity. Mandy and I are grateful that Andrew easily grasps language and readily adds new words to his growing vocabulary. When he was two I had asked him to remove a plastic bottle cap from his mouth.

"Daddy, it's not edible," he replied.

When I wondered in amazement where he had learned the word he said, "Mommy told me." I'm sure I was in high school before the word edible entered my vocabulary.

Brasstown Bald is 4,784 feet above sea level, which to Andrew's amazement is considerably taller than the Westin Peachtree Plaza. After our drive to North Georgia and our hike up Brasstown Bald, the temperature had fallen significantly. It was eighty-six degrees a hundred miles south in Atlanta, but only sixty-two degrees at the top of the mountain.

From the summit of the hotel it had seemed that we were on top of the world. Now, looking out from the visitor center's observation deck, we could see four states. We gazed at magnificent mountain ranges and spacious, lush valleys. Brasstown Bald has an interesting natural and cultural history of logging, farming, conservation and recreation. Andrew was most interested in the many helpful exhibits in the visitor center, especially a display about a refurbished 1900s logging train.

After a couple of hours we left the summit and hiked back to the parking area. "This time we'll have gravity on our side," I told Andrew, prompting much discussion on the way down.

"Daddy, if the earth is rotating so fast why don't we fall off?" he asked.

Roll the Windows Down, It's Raining

For the fun of it, from the parking lot we chose a different route home along Country Road 180. However, we had a valid concern. Could we travel through Helen without yielding to the call of the Chattahoochee River? Suddenly we heard a clap of thunder. "Roll the windows down, it's raining!" Andrew whooped.

We find it strange that many people let something as uncontrollable as the weather get them down. Most of us agree that sunny days are good, but see overcast and stormy days as bad. Georgia has been in a drought for a couple of years, but television and radio meteorologists still forecast rainy days with a sense of gloom as "inclement weather," and most people follow along without thinking.

"When did the rain that God sends to replenish the earth become inclement?" I wondered aloud. It's important to rise above perceived adversity. It's essential to find meaning, if not joy, in all of life. That's why when it rains we delight in rolling the windows down.

We had become hooked on tubing the Hooch. But we had already made plans to have dinner on our boat with Mandy. When we reached Helen, we opted for a late lunch at the Troll House Restaurant situated beneath the Helen Bridge. Watching people negotiating their tubes through the Chattahoochee's boulders and rapids, waving as if they knew we were members of the fraternity, I barely heard my cell phone ringing. Mandy advised that she would be home late. Apologizing, she suggested that we have dinner on our boat another night.

It was all Andrew and I needed. Wolfing down what remained of our shared meatball sub, we made our way to our favorite tubing station. Soon we were on the river whooping it up, chasing daylight in the frigid mountain water with only the last remaining rays of the waning sun to warm us.

Planning is important, but so is spontaneity. It is an important part of living every day well. Changing direction, expecting the unexpected and pursuing serendipity often leads to the most meaningful of life's treasures.

With Andrew napping, we continued our drive home. In the silence I reflected on my recent rereading of James Dobson's book, *Bringing Up Boys.* "There is no viable substitute for a dad making time to enjoy doing things with his son," Dobson had written.

Dobson also recommended another book dedicated to meaningful relationships between fathers and sons. *Daddy's Home,* by Greg Johnson and Mike Yorkey, offers these sobering observations:

- Parents having less time to spend with their families is the single-most-important reason for the family's decline in our society, according to a 1989 survey commissioned by the Massachusetts Mutual Insurance Company.

- The average five-year-old, we are told, spends twenty-five minutes a week in close interaction with his father, and twenty hours a week in close interaction with the TV. No wonder that in a recent survey of kindergartners and their priorities, Dad finished second to the boob tube.

I'm surprised that the father who shared only twenty-five minutes a week with his son finished as high as second on that survey. Clearly, the best thing we can give our children is ourselves. Love strengthened in the home will naturally lead to a desire for more – a child who is loved at home learns to love outside the home. The time we make for our children will in great degree determine the time they will make for us later in life. There is a minimum standard for a dad who wants to make a difference in his child's life. The minimum standard is to be home for dinner and to share bedtime rituals.

This still allows for a fifty-hour work week, if one is so inclined. But I know from personal experience that anything less than the minimum standard at home, and anything more than fifty hours a week at work, is detrimental to relationships and to physical and spiritual well being.

After hiking up and down Brasstown Bald, tubing on the Chattahoochee and driving more than two hundred miles that day, I was bone-weary and happy to be nearing home when Andrew woke.

"Daddy, can we wrestle before I go to sleep tonight?" he asked.

I thought about it, but only for a moment.

"Sure, and I'm gonna kick your butt!" I replied. In my mind I could hear Mandy.

"No bad words, please."

Praying for Cars

One of my part-time jobs while in college was unloading trucks. One night Tim, a co-worker, and I were carrying heavy boxes of television sets from a trailer. As we struggled to empty the trailer, Tim told me he needed a big car for his large family. When he asked if I would help him in praying for a Cadillac, I said I would. The next day he inquired about my prayer. I told Tim that I had prayed, but that God was more likely to help him purchase a pre-owned

Chevy or Ford.

A few days later, Tim wheeled into the parking lot in a late-model Cadillac. His uncle in Tennessee had called to let him know he was getting a new car, and he had offered Tim favorable terms on his two-year-old Caddy.

Later my friend Ken Cox told me a similar story. When Ken needed a new car for his growing family he and his wife, Kim, prayed for one. A couple of weeks later Ken went to a local Honda dealer, where an affable salesman brought forth a car meeting all of Ken's specifications.

"Mr. Cox, this is your car for only $14,000," said the salesman.

Ken looked the car over and assured the man it was just what he and Kim had prayed for. There's only one problem.

"God told me that car would cost $11,500," said Ken.

The salesman was incredulous, but Ken politely made it clear that his price was firm. Shaking his head, the salesmen excused himself and went to consult with his manager. Ken was not surprised when he returned. The dealer had agreed to sell the car for $11,500.

My own "praying for cars" story occurred soon after Andrew was born, when our family chariot began showing signs of a faulty transmission. I called a friend, Phil Cooke, who owns a General Motors dealership in Madison, and asked Phil to look for a good pre-owned, low-mileage car. I said that I was thinking about a Mercury Marquis. Phil replied that he was more likely to take in a Chevrolet on trade.

"Why a Marquis?" he asked.

"I've never owned a Mercury. I don't know anyone who owns a

Marquis, and I can't recall ever riding in one. But since Mandy and I prayed about it, I've been thinking about a Mercury Marquis." "What color have you been thinking about?" Phil asked, playing along.

"My preference is a white car with blue leather interior," I said optimistically.

Phil assured me that he would be mindful of my request, but said he was going on vacation for ten days. When he got back, he would call me about the next low-mileage trade-in he received. But he reiterated that it would most likely be a Chevy.

The transmission problems continued to worsen. The day before Phil left on vacation I took my car in for inspection by Wesley and Grant at Campbell Collision. They indicated the repair would cost more than the car was worth. My next stop was Day-Break, my men's Bible study at the Atlanta Athletic Club, where I offered an unspoken prayer. I didn't want people knowing that I was praying about a car – surely God had more important things to do.

I went for a second opinion. Dale at AAMCO echoed the guys at Campbell Collision, saying that my transmission was about to expire and suggesting that I get a new car soon. I decided to call Phil back to raise the level of urgency. When I returned to my car, there was a message from Mandy on my cell phone.

"Nick, call Phil Cooke. He needs to speak to you right away."

When I called Phil, we shared a laugh. My low-mileage Mercury Grand Marquis would be ready the next morning. An elderly couple had traded in the Marquis on a new van. They told Phil they'd been contemplating their purchase for months.

The next morning Mandy, Andrew and I drove to Madison. "What color is it?" Mandy asked.

"Phil didn't say, but I'm pretty sure it's white with blue leather interior."

Phil had already left on vacation, but he had made sure our car was detailed and looking like new. White with blue leather interior, it was waiting in front of the showroom.

When Phil returned, he called to inquire how I liked the car. I assured him that I was pleased, and asked, "Phil, when is the last time you took a Mercury Marquis in on trade?"

"I've thought about that, too," he replied. "I'm sure I must have, but I don't recall ever taking a Marquis in on trade."

Andrew and I find humor in stories like these. They cause me to rethink my stodgy beliefs about God's involvement in the affairs of mankind. The moral for our son was that prayer is often serious, but it can also be fun. God has a sense of humor, and nothing is too big or too small for His involvement.

Chapter Six

THE GIFT OF CONTENTMENT

Every day in a life fills the whole life with
expectation and memory.
- C.S. Lewis

It had been three months since I started my fifteen-month sabbatical. With one year to go and Andrew only two weeks away from his fifth birthday, I decided to sit down and take stock.

For the first time in more than thirty years I was unemployed. After thirty years of putting money away, it felt odd to use our savings and investments to pay the bills. Does a man just drop a lucrative career to spend fifteen months with his son?

Fortunately, I had stopped defining my life by my career and was confident in what I was doing. It felt good to spend more time with family and friends. It felt good to make more time to rest and read. I was sharing the adventure of life with my son, comfortable living in the present and planning for the future. I often thanked God, for I'd never been happier.

I knew that the opinion of others around me included both ends of the spectrum. Many people were supportive. They admired my decision to spend more time with Andrew, and with family and friends. They were happy for me. They wished me well.

Susan, Mandy's friend, had a different observation. A psychologist, she said I'd have difficulty separating my self-worth from my career. I'd miss the excitement of making important decisions and big bucks. I wasn't the type to spend hours and hours with a soon-to-be five-year-old.

Others were less forthright, but I could see in their faces what they were thinking. "Poor stiff. Can't find work."

I quickly learned not to tell people I was using the time away from work to write a book. If I didn't survive cancer, my journal would help Andrew know that his dad had loved him. It would give him the advice a dad must give his son. But whenever I had made the mistake of mentioning my book in the early days, the hesitant verbal response I received did little to hide a transparent skepticism. I could see them thinking, "Sure. And one of my paintings is hanging in the Guggenheim!"

While I had my own occasional concerns, deep down I knew I was doing the right thing and remained firm in my commitment. Without contentment in what we have, and in who we are, what's it all about? If those who love us are not there to share the joy when our ship comes in, are we a success? Contrary to Susan's observation, it was easy to stop defining myself by my career. I was having fun being with Andrew, and writing about it. In my new role I had found contentment.

Submarine Commander

There are three types of people in this world: Those who make things happen,   those who watch things happen, and those who wonder what happened.

- Mary Kay Ash

One bright Thursday in mid-August Andrew and I left the house early to avoid the morning rush hour. In one day we were going to visit a waterfall, a mountain top and a river.

On our drive to the waterfall Andrew asked if I'd tell him a story about a submarine. The tall tale developed as we drove, and I ended with a reprise of Bob Newhart's comical satire called the *Submarine Commander*:

> I'd like to congratulate you men. We cut two minutes off the previous record for surfacing, firing at our target, and re-submerging. I just want to congratulate you men on your teamwork. At the same time, I don't want in any way to slight the men that we had to leave on deck. I think they had a lot to do with the two minutes we cut off the record. I doubt that any of us will forget their stunned expressions as we watched them through the periscope.

I chuckled as I finished the story, but the humor escaped my son.

"Daddy, I don't think that's funny. What happened to the men on deck?"

After a weak attempt to explain the humor, I quickly changed course and assured Andrew that the men on deck had been rescued. It's a funny story, I thought, but I'll try again later in life. The moral for me, as every good comedian knows, is that humor, like life, has everything to do with timing and perspective.

Soon we were at High Shoals Falls. Relaxing on the observation platforms overlooking the two waterfalls on High Shoals Creek, we again shared the mesmerizing pleasure of having all our senses treated.

"The simple things in life are the most rewarding," I told Andrew. "What I help place in your heart is significantly more meaningful than anything I'll ever place in your hands."

Returning to the car thinking of Mandy at home, I asked Andrew what we should bring back from our visit to the falls. His response was testimony to our commitment to help keep our natural habitats clean. But it was not what I expected.

"Trash," he said.

Recovering from Peril

There are two types of people in your life; those who nourish you and those who drain you. (There are) those who help you grow and those who are toxic to your growth. Toxic draining people can drag down even the most determined positive person and cause you to fall short of your potential. Flee from them. Don't try to change them; change yourself, change friends.

- Les Brown

From the falls we took a circuitous route north to the beautiful Blue Ridge Mountains and were soon gazing over a fascinating expanse of the Appalachians. We could see forever. Savoring the variety of colors and shapes with a cool wind flowing through the trees, listening to the far-off calls of a hawk, Andrew wished that he, too, could ride effortlessly on the wind currents. Listening to a creek rushing below us, we breathed deeply of nature's bouquet – evergreen and clover aromas, therapeutic both to heart and soul – and agreed that some things are discernable only in mountain solitude.

There is no rushing through the steep, winding mountain roads of North Georgia. Occasionally we pulled over to visit points of interest. Buying a snack and drink at an old-time general store, we were served by a toothless attendant. We decided teeth are like family and friends: take care of them or lose them.

When we reached Helen in early afternoon Andrew asked if we could tube the Chattahoochee before lunch. I was pleased that he was more interested in an activity than a meal. Meals provide an important opportunity for families to spend time together, and so do activities. Americans spend far too much time eating poorly, and far too little time sharing play. Too much of our entertainment includes unhealthy foods, and too often we watch rather than do. We are fortunate to have so much, but we consume far more than we need.

Some popular diet plans discourage skipping meals, but I believe that adults should skip one meal a day to maintain a healthy weight. To motivate myself to skip a meal a day, I multiple the number of meals I skip each month by $5 and send that amount to one of my favorite charities. The meal we replace with a liter or two of clean water makes us healthier. When we are healthier we are happier, and this bodes well for our relationships as well as for other aspects of our lives.

I also recommend that adults take a serious look at kid's menus and dollar meals in restaurants. These meals provide healthier portions than most of the meals on the regular menu. At Wendy's, for example, a baked potato and juice or water, or a dollar cup of chili, is delicious, nutritious and cheap. With kid's meals, you get the added benefit of a small dessert along with a toy or some learning material. I love reading the learning material with Andrew, and often better understand things myself. But I'm sure you already know the name of the biggest animal to ever live.

Thirty years ago when I shot the Hooch with my daughters there were no companies renting bright pink and green tubes. Back then we visited the only gas station in town and asked the proprietor for a truck tube. He would look around the garage for a family-sized one, wash the dust off and fill it with air. Handing it to us he would say, "No charge. Just stop by the next time you need gas."

Now, some thirty years later, tubing the Hooch is big business. We made our way to the tubing station and for the bargain price of six dollars received two large green tubes. For the first time, Andrew wanted his own tube. On his first solo ride and gaining confidence, he hit a stretch of whitewater and tumbled overboard. His life vest kept him buoyant and safe, but nevertheless he quickly reached out and accepted my helping hand. As I lifted him out of the cold water he gave me a broad smile. "That was awesome!"

Laughing, we watched Andrew's empty tube hurrying down the river ahead of our slower, shared ride. I enjoy Andrews's great sense of humor and his ability to laugh at himself. I am also thankful that Andrew is an adventurous child, more likely to do something than to view something. When he asked me to repeat my observation of his white water plunge a couple of times, I was happy to oblige. Retelling stories where a child admirably recovers from "peril" builds confidence and strengthens courage.

Thirty yards ahead of us, a water snake slithered across the river. Andrew said that one of his friends had told him rattlesnakes are the most dangerous things in the world. He asked if it was true. I told him I thought negative people were far more dangerous than rattlesnakes. We discussed the dangers of pessimistic and grouchy people. Grouches refuse to take responsibility for their lives. They blame others for their unhappiness. A pessimist gets a clean bill of health at his annual physical and then wants a second opinion. We agreed to only cultivate the friendships of positive people who make good things happen.

Near the end of our float, grey clouds began gathering. By the time we reached the takeout location the low rumble of thunder was close at hand. Our warm, sunny day had been replaced by a surprising summer storm. As we sprang for the safety of shore, a loud thunderbolt crackled just over our heads.

"Daddy, don't worry. God will take care of us," Andrew assured me.

I agreed that He would, but suggested we swiftly find cover. When the ancient Blue Bird school bus arrived we darted on board along with a half-dozen teenagers. As hail began pelting down, Andrew and I helped raise the windows, some of which couldn't be closed. "It doesn't matter – we're already wet," said one of the teens, echoing our own philosophy about joyfully letting rain come into our lives.

On the way home we decided to have dinner at the Olive Garden. Andrew ordered one of his favorite meals, macaroni and cheese with extra broccoli, and we started a conversation with a couple at an adjacent table. We had more than enough in common with Tom and Harriet to enjoy a lively dinner conversation. I watched with amusement as Tom observed Andrew's disappearing pile of broccoli. At the end of the meal Harriet was amazed. "Andrew, what have you done with your broccoli?" she asked.

Back on the road, Andrew dozed off while I thought about Tom and Harriet. I could just hear them talking about us in their own car. "Can you believe the kid ate that whole plate of broccoli?"

Meanwhile, I had enjoyed a wonderful meal chosen off the kid's menu. And by the way, if you guessed that the biggest animal to ever live was a Tyrannosaurus Rex, you may guess again. A blue whale is the biggest animal that ever lived.

Follow Your Dream

> *A study conducted on three thousand high achievers from around the world concluded that the common denominator was not sky-high intelligence. The study found that eighty-five per cent of the three thousand high achievers had achieved their goals in life because of their attitude, and only fifteen per cent of them because of their aptitude.*
>
> *- Les Brown*

One Sunday after church Mandy decided to take Andrew and a neighbor's child to the park. They returned sooner than anticipated, having already dropped the neighbor's son off at home. "Too crowded?" I asked.

"No," Mandy replied. "Tommy (name changed to protect the crabby) complained the whole time so we decided to come home."

Mandy and I have had other conversations about Tommy's controlling grumbling, but this time we realized that our community involvement with Tommy's parents was the cause of our invitations to play with Andrew. We decided that we weren't being fair to our son. We needed some time away from the tiny pessimist, and from his parents.

Talking to Mandy about Tommy reminded me of Ben Barnes, the son of our good friends Jared and Katherine Knott. Ben's first father died when he was young, but Jared is an excellent dad. Ben was the first hearing-impaired Eagle Scout in the state of Georgia, and he is an inspiration to everyone who has the good fortune to know him.

A tall, good-looking young man, Ben loves our restored red 1973 Mustang convertible. When Ben was in high school I told him he could use the Mustang for his senior prom. He proudly used the car to drive his beautiful date to the formal event.

There is no evidence that Ben's hearing impairment and related speech difficulty has, or ever will, negatively affect his successful life. This became apparent a few summers ago. Ben left home one morning advising his mom that he was off to find a job. Katherine, who is somewhat protective, attempted to persuade her ambitious son to stay home, but he was already out the door looking for work.

On a hunch, Ben approached a groundskeeper at the nearby Sugarloaf Country Club. With difficulty, he asked the man if there was anything he could do to help out. The man looked the physically fit teen over and replied, "Yes, there is."

Ben began laboring on the links. Despite his impairments his great smile, positive attitude and diligence were soon noticed. A few days later the head groundskeeper asked, "Who's the kid?"

"I don't know. I thought you sent him to me," responded the man who had given Ben the work.

Mulling over the situation, they decided Ben deserved compensation for his labor. They had no trouble collecting a cash bounty from the dozen other workers, and soon they hired Ben on staff. He worked there for the balance of that summer, and for every summer afterward until he went away to college.

"Daddy," Andrew asked me one day. "Will Ben ever have full hearing and speech?"

I told Andrew I thought that one day he might, but if not I was confident that Ben would continue to mature into a successful man.

The Main Thing

What is a success?
To laugh often and much;
To win the respect of intelligent people and the affection of children;
To earn the appreciation of honest critics and endure the betrayal of false friends;
To appreciate beauty;
To find the best in others;
To leave the world a bit better, whether by a healthy child, a garden patch of a redeemed social condition;
To know even one life has breathed easier because you have lived;
That is to have succeeded.

- Ralph Waldo Emerson

Nobel Prize author Aleksandr Solzhenitsyn courageously lived under the tyranny of Joseph Stalin's communism and spent many years in the dehumanizing Gulag Archipelago. But Solzhenitsyn prevailed to become a world-renowned author. His insightful writings include prophetic advice that even a child can comprehend.

What about the main thing in life, all its riddles? If you want, I'll spell it out for you right now. Do not pursue what is illusory – property and position: all that is gained at the expense of your nerves decade after decade, and is confiscated one fell night. Live with a steady superiority over life – don't be afraid of misfortune and do not yearn after happiness. Our envy of others devours us most of all. Rub your eyes and purify your heart – and prize above all else in the world those who love you and wish you well.

Andrew's favorite literature is still about Thomas, Scooby, Arthur and Franklin, so I fully understand why some people may find it premature for us to include Aleksandr Solzhenitsyn in his repertoire of bedtime books. But it is never too soon to read to a child from great works that cultivate character. When is a child too young to understand that he is loved and valued?

Chapter Seven

GREYHOUND EXPRESS

There are only two lasting bequests we can hope to give our children. One of these is roots; the other is wings.

- Hodding Carter

For weeks we had been planning a Greyhound bus jaunt to visit Nanny, Granddad and Emily in South Carolina. At the end of August our departure date finally arrived, and Andrew was beside himself with excitement.

Mandy and I are fortunate to have loving families, even though we are all a bit nutty. Mandy's mother and father live in the congenial revolutionary war town of Camden, South Carolina, as do Tracy and Doug Bell, her sister and brother-in-law, and their daughter Emily. Emily was born a couple of weeks after Andrew, and they share a strong bond. The prospect of seeing Emily again added greatly to Andrew's excitement.

We purchased express tickets with one stop in Augusta, Georgia on our way to Columbia, the capital of South Carolina, where the Marshalls would meet us for the drive to Camden. I was a little disappointed with our itinerary – a couple of additional stops in historic towns along the way would have added to our adventure. Nevertheless, we boarded our bus smiling with anticipation, and settled into adjoining seats.

"Why is it called a Southeast Stage Bus? Where will it end up? Where are all these other people headed?" Andrew's first long-distance bus ride began with a string of questions. I was happy to add Greyhound buses to the growing list of Andrew's transportation experiences.

My initial disappointment at having only one rest stop turned into concern when the driver announced that our first halt would be in Athens, home of the University of Georgia. I checked our tickets – sure enough, our first and only stop should be Augusta. Making my way to the front of the bus, I pondered the sage advice to "be careful of what you wish." However, the driver confirmed that we were on the right bus and that we would eventually arrive in Columbia.

I told Andrew my findings. There were more stops than we had anticipated. We would have rest stops in Athens and Augusta and shorter stops in Washington, Fort Gordon and Thompson, Georgia, then another short stop in Aiken, South Carolina. Andrew thought for a moment and with a child's wonderful perspective asked, "Do we have to pay more?"

We reveled in our good fortune. It is not often these days that we get more than we bargain for, particularly at no additional cost. Avoiding much of the heavy traffic on Interstate 20, the bus proceeded along the picturesque byways of highways 316 and 78 through rural towns and pastoral hues of brown and green. We watched soft white clouds effortlessly floating across the blue sky. Even with the windows closed, wonderful fragrances of freshly mowed grass and country clover rewarded our senses. It was easy to visually and mentally absorb the beauty of our surroundings.

At Fort Gordon, a United States army base near Augusta, the driver advised all passengers to have identification in hand. As we approached the main gate, a security officer boarded the bus. Andrew watched wide-eyed as the officer asked three men to leave. Without proper identification, they would have to wait at the gate for the bus to return after visiting Fort Gordon. The short ride from the gate to the Greyhound station was replete with intriguing sights – security gates, checkpoints with gun-toting officers, soldiers, tanks, a helicopter and a fire station – all of which fired Andrew's imagination, and all at no additional cost!

After our visit to Fort Gordon we began reminiscing about my own military days, including the two years I had spent in England. I told Andrew about seeing the smoke emanating from chimneys in the modest English village and farmhouses surrounding the base of RAF Chicksands. My four years in the United States Air Force had been a positive experience. I felt good about serving my country, but fours years of regimentation were enough for my unregimented soul. I had accepted my honorable discharge with gratitude, and had found it easy to trade in my uniform for more choices in civilian life.

"Daddy, can we visit Chicksands one day?" Andrew pleaded. Mandy had already visited the base with me on our honeymoon, but I assured Andrew that we would add it to our list. The three of us would one day visit Chicksands.

As we neared Augusta I pointed out the renowned Augusta National Golf Club where earlier that year Mandy's mom and I had watched Tiger Woods win the Masters. The Masters was one of the most exciting sporting events of my life. I'm not a golfer but being at the Masters rivaled being at a Super Bowl, a World Series game or a championship NASCAR race.

Expensive Care

After leaving Augusta I suggested a nap, and Andrew went out like Sonny Liston in a Mohammad Ali fight. Looking at his sleeping face and easing into my own restful meditation, I remembered visiting a neighbor recently at Joan Glancy Hospital. Richard was recovering from an accident. As we entered his room he gave us a welcoming smile, glad to see us and pleased that he'd just been moved out of intensive care. Andrew's concern was obvious. The doctor removing belts and tubes from his patient assured Andrew that Richard was going to be okay now that he was out of intensive care.

On the way home, Andrew was quiet. Mandy was preparing dinner as we entered the house.

"How's Richard?" she asked.

"Okay now that he's out of expensive care," Andrew replied.

Perfectly Unrefined

On the bus, two elderly women in front of us were conversing. Many of their homespun observations caught my ear.

"Having large breasts is only good for a short time before gravity gets 'em."

"I've never seen a healthy looking person in a health food store."

"Most of these women complaining about sexual harassment need a good hug."

"The good thing about getting older is you can keep a secret 'cause you forget things easy."

"Most people trying to sound intelligent are stupid."

The latter comment was my favorite. The younger of the two offered the older woman some left-over chicken and vegetables she had bought at the ancient Augusta rest-stop cafeteria. The older women politely told her friend that she never ate food from small, out-of-the-way places because she had read that they were not well-regulated and were far more likely to have poorly prepared food. For this very reason, she said, in the United States there is now a rise in semolina deaths.

The humorous homespun philosophy of these ladies was largely based on common sense, but something in that last statement didn't fit. In my restful state, however, I couldn't quite put my finger on it. Pondering this question while gazing out the bus window, I saw our reception party. We were in Columbia. Soon we were caught up in the fun of our welcome. After that we ate dinner in Columbia, talked in the car on the way to Camden and enjoyed ice cream at the Marshall's home, where the kids played while the adults caught up on family news. It all made for an exciting evening. It wasn't until later in bed that I chuckled, realizing what hadn't fit in the ladies' conversation on the bus.

Eating in out-of-the-way restaurants doesn't cause death by semolina. Semolina is pasta. What we should fear is salmonella.

My father's formal training didn't go any further than grade school, but he encouraged his three children to get a good education. He wanted us to establish careers and to enjoy our lives. I believe that is the desire of all good parents. It's why Mandy and I always make time to explain the meaning of a new word to Andrew, repeating the word for clarity, using it in a sentence and confirming that he is comfortable adding it to his ever-growing vocabulary. At the rate we are progressing, I'm quite sure that by the time he enters third grade Andrew will have successfully absorbed my entire spoken lexicon.

I occasionally watch game shows and am generally favorably impressed with how quickly the contestants answer questions. Even when I know the answer, I often need a bit of time to respond. Andrew responds without much deliberation, probably because he has a good memory. One of my least-favorite comments from him, particularly when he is right, which is most of the time, is, "I thought you said...."

Andrew's older sisters were the same way. When we lived in Miami Dawn had filled our home with neighborhood children eager to learn in her "classroom." Kimberly had succeeded Dawn in attracting eager-to-learn kids on Saturday mornings. Even back then both girls had found pleasure in teaching, so it is no surprise that today both my daughters excel in their vocation of choice, teaching.

That night Cousin Emily joined Andrew in my attentive audience for bedtime reading. We normally read for pleasure, and whenever possible I include life lessons. By popular request, I read C. S. Lewis' observation:

> Very often the only way to get a quality in reality is to start behaving as if you had it already. That is why children's games are so important. They are always pretending to be grown-ups—playing soldiers, playing shop. But all the time, they are hardening their muscles and sharpening their wits, so that the pretense of being grown-ups helps them grow up in earnest.

Reading C.S. Lewis led to a discussion about understanding how to find purpose in life. The two children were intrigued to hear again that their God-given talents make them special. They wanted to know what talents they had been given. What did I think their talents were? How many talents did they have?

I explained that the wonderful imaginations of children, including their games, are important aspects of growing up. How gratifying and encouraging it was for Emily and Andrew to understand that playing – yes, playing! – is not only fun, but it is an important aspect of learning.

We tend to assume that the meaning of life must be mysterious and complicated, but with their uninhibited faith and optimism, most children are well-suited to discover their own talents and purpose.

They do so in the natural flow of life.

What an adult accomplishes in life has much to do with what the parents nurtured and encouraged. The progress of mankind is inextricably connected to the ability of children to realize their aspirations. Children reach for the stars; most adults no longer see them. It all starts with making time for those who we are trusted to parent.

Fred and the Raincoat

"Daddy, before we go to sleep can you tell us just one more story?" asked Andrew. "Can you tell Emily about Fred and the raincoat?"

It was a reasonable request, and one that fit well within our discussion about being uniquely blessed. Fred Wirt is a special person. He is about my age, and we have been friends for more than thirty years.

Early in our friendship Fred had asked if I thought he was different. "Do people think I'm stupid?" he asked. "Sometimes people make fun of me because I still live with my parents, because I don't drive a car and I clean houses for my job. Some people think I'm strange."

"Fred," I replied, "I believe most people look at you and me and think 'What's a bright guy like Fred doing with a bumpkin like Nick?'"

Laughing, I observed that my reply wasn't exactly an endorsement of him, and that he might want to set a higher standard for his friendships. Fortunately, Fred and his parents have remained my friends for many years and I now have many rewarding stories about "Fredrick the Great."

Andrew and Emily especially wanted to hear the one about Fred and the raincoat. Tucking them under the covers, I began by telling them about my new Burberry trench coat. During my clothes-hog days, I was more likely to buy new threads based upon desire than need. Whenever I had indulged in my urge, I'd magnanimously pass along the clothes I didn't need to Fred or, if Fred wasn't interested, to Goodwill. My new trench coat was a chic – and totally unnecessary – replacement for a hardly used, still-fashionable London Fog raincoat.

I drove by Fred's home to pick him up for a clam-and-chicken-wing dinner at Tarks on Federal Highway near Fort Lauderdale. One of our favorite eateries, it is a funky place where most clients sit on a stool within reach of the cook. A sign over the deep-fryers reads: "Food cooked in sight must be right." Another sign reads: "No shirt, no shoes, no problem."

Many patrons were in compliance with the latter sign. In Tarks, tattoos are far more prevalent than ties, and no one much cares about cholesterol or calories. No silverware is delivered with the meals, and if you ask for some it's obvious you don't belong.

Everywhere Fred goes he is a catalyst for animated conversation and laughter. Anticipating our feast of clams and wings and exchanging greetings with the other patrons, we bellied up to the counter. Fred was celebrating his new job at Winn Dixie. Because he now had to travel further, however, the main topic of our conversation was a new bicycle to replace Fred's dated wheels.

After too many deep-fried creatures and flappers we high-fived our way out of Tarks and carried our bloated bellies to Wal-Mart. It didn't take long for Fred to decide on a package deal that included a bike, basket, horn and headlight, all on sale. There was only one problem. He wanted the floor model.

Assuring the salesman that I was a loyal customer and a longtime shareholder, I mentioned that Sam Walton and I had been quite close at one time. The salesman politely excused himself. I thought perhaps I'd gone too far, anxiously imagining him in the back room calling Bentonville. I did have a sincere admiration for the founder of Wal-Mart, and had once sat close to him on a flight. I had always felt that Mr. Walton and I were cut from the same cloth – give or take several billion dollars.

The salesmen soon returned, and to my great relief he agreed to make an exception to store policy by selling us the floor model. We avoided the unenviable task of assembling the bike and accessories. My inability to put things together, even with instructions, which I invariably save until all else fails, is legendary. Had I retained all of the nuts, bolts and other parts left over from assembling swing sets, doll houses and various mail order items from Dawn and Kimberly's childhood, today I'd have a lucrative parts business.

Andrew and Emily were sleepy, but excited for Fred. With his new bike secured in the trunk of my car, Fred and I made our way to my house so I could give him my scarcely worn London Fog raincoat. Entering my walk-in closet, we saw the two garments hanging side by side. Looking at them, Fred inquired as to which was his. I assured him that the London Fog coat was almost new. Pensively studying them, Fred observed that the most sincere form of giving is when it involves what we value most.

My well-read friend and I discussed this for a while, until I realized that it was getting late. I needed to get Fred home. I handed him the Burberry. In the car we sat silently for a few minutes, then Fred asked if I felt bad about giving him my new coat.

I thought for a few moments. I wanted to provide an honest answer, and a part of me did feel bad. Then I responded.

"Fred, I did the right thing and I learned a couple of valuable lessons. We shouldn't buy things we don't need, and there is no honor in giving what we don't want."

At the end of my story, Andrew asked his attentive cousin if she knew the moral of the story. Emily matter-of-factly responded.

"Sure. Fred is smarter than Uncle Nick!"

Chapter Eight

IF

*Give me the children until they are seven, and anyone may
have them afterwards.*
- *St. Francis Xavier*

Andrew's first day of pre-school was coming up. Coincidentally, it
would commence on September 6, his fifth birthday. To prepare, we
visited Pleasant Hill Pre-school where we attended an open house
and met his teacher, Miss Anita, and Jean Fitzpatrick, the headmaster. They appeared to be caring people, and we added them to our
nightly prayers.

At the orientation we learned with dismay that the standard pre-school schedule required attendance from 8 am to noon on Monday,
Wednesday and Friday, or the same hours on Tuesday and Thursday.
Sadly, I pictured the fifteen-month adventure Andrew and I were
sharing being hampered. I decided to approach the school to see if
anything could be done.

Headmaster Jean Fitzpatrick at first rejected my request to adjust
Andrew's schedule. As I explained our mission, however, she began
to listen with interest. Soon she became enthusiastic about the value

Andrew was gaining from our outings. The clincher came when I outlined our plan to visit the Okefenokee National Wildlife Refuge. She agreed to make an exception.

With Andrew now attending pre-school on Monday, Tuesday and Wednesday mornings, we'd still have Wednesday afternoons, Thursdays, Fridays and some weekends to continue our adventure. Next year he would begin attending formal kindergarten five days a week from 9 am to 3 pm.

On his first day of pre-school we lingered over breakfast on our porch, watching songbirds diving onto our feeders and talking about school, and the fun of growing up. I told him how excited Mandy and I were about the fun he would have. Before leaving for her own school day, Mandy had given Andrew a big hug and wished him well. On the short drive to pre-school, I could feel his excitement mounting.

Pulling into the parking lot, I was grateful for the line of cars ahead of us. It would give us a little more time together. Waiting in the lineup, witnessing Andrew's healthy mix of excitement and concern, a host of emotions welled up in me. We know our kids must grow up, and we want them to, but part of us doesn't want to let them go. Part of us wants to protect them from life's vicissitudes. We let them go a little at a time.

When our turn came, Andrew hopped from the car. Grasping his first teacher's hand, he disappeared behind the double doors leading to the start of his formal education.

Running Against the Wind

The ultimate measure of a man is not where he stands in moments of comfort and convenience, but where he stands at times of challenge and controversy.
> *- Martin Luther King, Jr.*

Watching Andrew begin this new phase of life, I remembered Dawn and Kimberly's first day of school along with an earlier learning experience they had shared one afternoon many years before. When the girls were just a bit older than Andrew is now, I had taken them to an open field near our home to fly their first kite. As we assembled our contraption with its fragile smiley-face fabric-covered wood frame and tail made of rags, the girl's excitement grew.

"Please Dad, let us fly it ourselves," they pleaded.

It was a windy day. Knowing they would have difficulty launching the kite without help, I decided to let them try anyway. What I didn't anticipate was that they would attempt to raise the kite by running *with* the wind. After several attempts, the kite was becoming tattered and the frustration level of the girls was growing.

"Come help us, Daddy," Dawn implored. "We're hopeless."

Observing me sprinting against the wind, they quickly realized their mistake. They tried again, and this time the smiley-face kite began tugging on its tether string as it rose gracefully into the spacious sky. The girls squealed with excitement as it reached heights they hadn't anticipated. They took turns holding the string. It was an exciting day.

Every productive life is filled with challenges. Our lives are defined not by avoiding adversity, but by how we deal with it. Kites rise not with, but against, the wind.

What We Think is Important

Children have never been very good at listening to their elders, but they have never failed to imitate them.

- James Baldwin

Twenty minutes early to pick up Andrew, I was first in the car pool line. He entered the car smiling, and it was obvious he'd had a good morning. He was pleased with himself and elated about socializing and learning with the other children. Over lunch at the Chick-Fil-A playground, listening to him tell about his first day of school, I realized there was no need for concern. Our son was going to do well.

That evening I began reading Rudyard Kipling's popular poem *If*. Written in 1895, it evokes Victorian stoicism and the stiff-upper-lip philosophy of popular British culture.

> If you can keep your head when all about you
> Are losing theirs and blaming it on you;
> If you can trust yourself when all men doubt you,
> But make allowance for their doubting too:
> If you can wait and not be tired by waiting,
> Or being lied about, don't deal in lies,
> Or being hated, don't give way to hating,
> And yet don't look too good, nor talk too wise;
> If you can dream—and not make dreams your master;
> If you can think—and not make thoughts your aim,
> If you can meet with Triumph and Disaster
> And treat those two imposters just the same:
> If you can bear to hear the truth you've spoken
> Twisted by knaves to make a trap for fools,
> Or watch the things you gave your life to, broken,
> And stoop and build 'em up with worn-out tools;
> If you can make one heap of all your winnings
> And risk it on one turn of pitch-and-toss,
> And lose, and start again at your beginnings
> And never breathe a word about your loss:
> If you can force your heart and nerve and sinew
> To serve your turn long after they are gone,
> And so hold on when there is nothing in you
> Except the Will which says to them: "Hold on!"
> If you can talk with crowds and keep your virtue,
> Or walk with Kings – nor lose the common touch,

If neither foes nor loving friends can hurt you,
If all men count with you, but none too much:
If you can fill the unforgiving minute
With sixty seconds' worth of distance run,
Yours is the Earth and everything that's in it,
And – which is more – you'll be a Man, my son!

– Rudyard Kipling

Andrew asked if we could read *If* together at bedtime. But first he wanted to watch his favorite movie. Andrew enjoys *What About Bob?* (a family-friendly version) with Bill Murray and Richard Dreyfuss so much that his sisters gave him the DVD for Christmas. Watching the 1991 movie for what seemed like the hundredth time; we laughed and laughed in all the same places. Andrew has an infectious laugh, and sharing the lighter side of life with our son delights Mandy and me.

As Andrew and I prayed at bedtime, he reminded me to read *If* to him. After observing Mandy and I reading all his life, he has developed a strong interest in literature. He wouldn't accept my advice that Kipling's great work is better suited for later in life, so while reading the poem I added a bit of commentary that I thought would be suitable for a brand-new five-year-old. This is what I told my son:

"What we think is important, but only if we take action."

"What we do with our lives – like studying in school and how we treat people – will determine the kind of person we become."

"No one cares what we think unless they know we care."

"We must make time to listen to others."

After listening to my fatherly wisdom, Andrew sleepily rolled over and mumbled something. Leaning forward, I strained to hear his words. "Daddy, next time please get *If* with pictures."

Happy Fifth Birthday

The Southeastern Railway Museum located on thirty-four acres in Duluth, Georgia rewards both the old and the young – adults can reminisce about the good old days and children are exuberantly fascinated by the antique railroad displays. The museum hosts many special events such as its annual Father's Day Brunch, and it is a unique place for fun birthday parties.

Mandy invited two dozen family and friends to celebrate Andrew's fifth birthday in an historic train car. In the car we played games and bobbed for apples while a steam-engine video ran in the background. Scampering around the museum, the children explored a rich variety of classic locomotives, restored cabooses and historic Pullman cars.

The much-anticipated finale to the day was an actual ride in a restored red caboose pulled by an aging steam engine. The best part was when the engineer invited the birthday boy to ride up front in the locomotive. Twice Andrew was allowed to pull the steam-powered whistle before we returned to the station. Watching the broad smile on my son's face as we disembarked, an even bigger smile spread across my own. It would have been hard to tell who was happier.

The best bonds between father and son often form in a childlike sense of excitement for the simple things in life. Traveling beyond the horizon in imagination and in deed encourages a child – and the child in a man – to appreciate what he has.

Who to Contact in an Emergency

When Miss Anita, Andrew's new teacher, learned of his affinity for trains she sent home an article from the local paper about a model railroad exhibit at Vines Botanical Gardens.
The following Sunday Andrew and I decided to drive to the gardens in Loganville via the historic towns of Duluth and Lawrenceville.

Mandy had volunteered to help after church teaching children in Sunday school, and we agreed to meet back home for dinner.

Driving to Loganville, Andrew remembered something that had puzzled him at his doctor's appointment the previous Friday. We had gone for a couple of pre-school vaccinations. Taking our seats on the waiting-room sofa, we had been forced to endure an usually long sojourn. A couple arrived and with some degree of exasperation sat down to complete the multi-question application. I was tickled by a remark made by the husband, and Andrew observed my amusement with a degree of puzzlement.

"Daddy, remember in the doctor's office when you laughed with the people?"

"Yes."

"What were you laughing about?"

I explained that people get tired of filling out forms in doctor's waiting rooms. As the couple across from us was completing the long and repetitive questionnaire, the husband had pointed to one question in particular.

"What do they want here?" he asked.

"They want to know who to contact in an emergency," his wife replied.

Her husband exploded. "We're in a damned doctor's office and they want to know who to contact in an emergency?"

After I finished laughing, we again cooled our heels. I amused myself by envisioning a large waiting room outside the Pearly Gates. The only people in the room were doctors feverishly completing reams of information. A surly receptionist occasionally opened an opaque sliding window to hand out more forms or to collect a payment. The person who had been in the waiting room the longest observed that people were called for their appointments only after they had left to go to the restroom.

A doctor friend took exception to my imagery. He said there ought to be such a waiting room for lawyers. I agreed.

"What does the lawyer's waiting room look like?" he asked.

"Actually, they have two. One is outside the Pearly Gates and the other is a significant distance away."

"So the attorneys are burdened with relentless cross examination?"

"No. The room in the far distance is overcrowded with endless, noisy bickering. The room outside the Pearly Gates is empty."

Vines Botanical Gardens and Model Railroad

Vines Botanical Gardens is a beautiful twenty-five acre estate with picturesque trees, bushes and other appealing plant life. It features a serene lake complete with a pair of grown black swans. After a hasty retreat up the embankment, pecking swans in hot pursuit, Andrew and I can attest to the warning that you should not pet, feed or otherwise attempt contact with swans. Our advice is to just leave them be – some things in life are better appreciated from a safe distance.

Over the years our family has celebrated many family birthdays at the Vines restaurant, and we were disappointed when it closed. The manor house, an elegant 18,000-square-foot structure, now caters to private parties and weddings. It won't surprise me if Kimberly chooses the manor house for her wedding reception. It is a special place.
At the south end of the gardens, the Georgia Garden Railroad Society displays a number of interesting model trains and miniature

villages. From spring through fall, weather permitting, they set up every Sunday from 11 am to 3 pm.

A half-dozen neighborly gentlemen were in the early stages of setting up their train display. Resting his elbows on one of the bridge railings, Andrew placed his chin in his hands and remained intently silent for several minutes, watching a steam engine and a diesel locomotive running in different directions on separate tracks, pulling a variety of cars through the miniature villages. One of the gentlemen, Bob Giselbach, broke Andrew's attentive quietude with a warm smile.

"Okay, guys, what do you want to know?" he asked.

Andrew and I did have questions, and what Bob couldn't answer his associates from the Georgia Garden Railroad Society addressed most satisfactorily. Like virtually every train person we've ever met, the men were cordial and helpful. We spent two fascinating hours watching the trains and interacting with the men. The camaraderie, fun and education was much appreciated. Even better, our rewarding couple of hours came at no cost – the display had no entry fee. Wholeheartedly thanking our hosts, we assured them that we'd be back.

Cotton Candy and Blue Lips

Driving home through Loganville I turned on the radio. Listening to the Atlanta Braves pre-game show reminded me of a baseball game we had attended earlier in the summer at Turner Field.

We had treated Granddad and Cousin Emily. Arriving at Turner Field early, we found our seats over the Braves bullpen and stocked up on munchies. It was one of those times when healthy choices just weren't available, so we made the best of it with burgers, dogs, fries and beverages, festively passing the food around and laughing in anticipation of the game. Vendors offered a variety of other treats, including pink and blue cotton candy, and after much pleading we succumbed. The kid's beverage of choice was a colored snow cone called a blue icy that, much to their delight, immediately turned their lips, teeth and tongues a bright blue.

We were seated in the first row of the second level, directly behind the Braves bullpen. Granddad told Emily and Andrew that we were in good position to catch a home-run ball. Andrew thought for a moment.

"How will we give them their ball back?" he asked.

"You get to keep the ball as a souvenir – you don't have to return it," Granddad assured my puzzled son.

"But how will they play if we keep their ball?"

One hot dog, one blue icy, one bag of peanuts and one huge cotton candy into the game, a capricious summer storm let loose. We headed for cover but after thirty minutes of steady rain decided against waiting any longer. After running in the rain to our car just across Hank Aaron Boulevard, we drove back to Berkeley Lake with Emily and Andrew dozing under a beautiful rising full moon.

"I think the Braves should sell preferred seating for five-year olds," I chuckled. "It could be facing the parking lot as long as the venders kept coming with hot dogs, cotton candy and blue icies."

Granddad laughed. As we drove home, the kids slept and the moon rose on our day of simple pleasures.

The Boy Within

Back at home we woke the kids to brush their teeth and change into pajamas. In the process they recaptured enough energy to request a bedtime story. I asked what they wanted to hear.

"Let's talk about our bus trip," Andrew suggested.

"No, I don't want to hear about your old bus trip," retorted Emily. "My mom said Uncle Nick is nuts for riding the bus."

Amused by her remark, I made a suggestion. "Emily, please say that again over breakfast."

Andrew readily agreed to talk about our bus trip another time in favor of reading from a recent gift book, *101 Things You Should Do Before Going To Heaven*, by David Borden and Tom Winter. Intrigued by the title, Emily wanted to hear more.

It seemed appropriate, especially after Emily's earlier comment about our bus ride, to read the part entitled *Take a Retro Road Trip*. With both tots lying prostrate, elbows on bed and chins in palms, I began reading.

> *"What's the difference between a road trip and a car trip?*
>
> *"Attitude. A car trip is simply a means of getting from one place to another in as little time as possible."*

Interrupting, Emily asked why I liked doing kid stuff with her and Andrew. As I was still gathering my thoughts, Andrew answered.

"Because my dad is still a kid!"

"Uncle Nick isn't a kid," my niece giggled. "He even has gray hair."

"I am so a kid!"

I suggested that we get back to our reading. It was late, and the biggest kid in the room was tired.

My observant son was right. One way a man stops living is by giving up the boy within. When a man gives up the child in him, he abandons some of the wonderment and adventure of life. Dreams and aspirations that in our youth gave us so much creative energy are too often dulled by overscheduled obligation. We "safely" settle for less, and subsequently we steer our children away from their own dreams.

Nurturing the child within makes a man more interested, and interesting. When we nurture our inner child we tend to spend more time with our families – not because we should, but because we want to. The inner child lets us dream and take risks, so that we may become what God would have us be.

May we share the fate of Olympian Eric Liddell in feeling God's pleasure. The subject of the movie *Chariots of Fire, Liddell* was a Scottish theology student who trained for the 100-meter running event in the 1924 Olympics in Paris, but when the event was scheduled for a Sunday he refused to run in it. Steadfast in his belief that he should honor the Lord's Day, he decided to compete instead in the 400-meter event, for which he had not trained. He not only won a gold medal in the 400-meter event, but he broke the world and Olympic records.

Before the 1924 Olympics his sister had reminded Eric that they were a family of missionaries. She had suggested he give up running and his quest for Olympic gold. Eric's response was thoughtful. "I believe God made me for a purpose, but he also made me fast. And when I run I feel His pleasure."

What more could a person want? What more can a parent want, than that his child feels God's pleasure? Glancing down at Andrew and Emily, I continued reading.

"Unlike a car trip, a road trip is all about the journey. The joy is getting into the car and heading down an unfamiliar road, preferably one far away from the interstate, to see what you can see. No time schedules. No agendas. No speeding tickets. Just

looking out the window and stopping to explore when the urge arises.

"A retro road trip goes a step further. It means meandering through the miles without the diversion of the radio, CD player, or DVDs for the kids. Instead, it's just you, the open road, and the companionship and conversation of those you love, including your heavenly Father."

I'm convinced that even in slumber kids hear us reading to them, so as heads slipped from hands and two of my favorite people went calmly into the night, I finished the story.

"The less desperate you are to be entertained every waking minute, the more enjoyment you'll find in the simple things."

The next morning I'd forgotten all about my suggestion, but over breakfast Emily remembered to repeat her mom's remark. Everyone shared a good laugh as Tracey stammered to explain why she thought Uncle Nick was nuts to ride the bus.

Chapter Nine

THE BOY WITHIN

I was thinking about how the status symbol of today is a cell phone, but I can't afford one. So I'm wearing my garage door opener.
- Anonymous

Buckled in his car seat, Andrew was connecting matching vowel sounds, checking his homework. In the car-pool lane waiting for pre-school to open, we were chatting about our upcoming trip to the Okefenokee National Wildlife Refuge, but a woman behind us kept yelling at me to move forward.

"You have to move forward!" she shouted. "The sooner, the better!"

It was raining, a cordially cool September morning. Moving forward would have put us beyond the covered area. Weighing my options, I ventured a concerned glance in the rearview mirror.

My concern deepened when I realized the woman wasn't hollering at me. Instead, she was barking into her cell phone. Although relieved that I wasn't the target of her wrath, I felt a sense of sorrow for her daughter, who was languishing beside her with a blank stare. The mother-daughter disconnect was haunting.

The petite five-year-old appeared sad, perhaps contemplating spending hours away from home with a dozen new classmates she hardly knew. Adjusting her unfamiliar backpack, she could hardly zip it up. She looked worried that she might lose a front tooth eating a snack while her self-absorbed mother babbled on the flip phone.

Knowing how much Andrew and I enjoy our conversations, the empty gaze of the girl stayed with me and became a nagging image. After that, I noticed several moms and dads who regularly spoke on their cell phones for the ten or fifteen minutes that we waited for pre-school to open. I remembered when I prided myself on being so available to my associates. How many of these calls were little more than whining sessions on matters I had little or no control over? These calls were from people doing far better in life than the average person, but every time I met one need, they always reached into their inexhaustible bag for another, unnecessarily sacrificing time with their families and wanting me to do the same. The squeaky wheel does often get the grease, and whiners do often get their way, but at what cost to everyone around them?

Today I occasionally see these same people at social functions, but now I am thankful they can no longer require anything of me. They have a home, or two or three, along with luxury cars and the latest and greatest of gadgets, but I see emptiness in their eyes. Contentment is elusive for the self-absorbed. Watching the little girl in the car behind us staring blankly out the window, I pledged to teach Andrew to avoid self-absorbed people whenever possible, and to set limits if the interaction cannot be avoided.

When mothers and fathers are too busy to share a few minutes with their children, they forever forfeit that time. Children are our messengers, our emissaries to the future. Thoughtful dialogue, even for only a few minutes at a time, helps fortify our caring commitment. What child (and what adult, for that matter) doesn't need reminders that he or she is loved?

In Harry Chapin's foreboding warning, the cycle of neglect starts with a preoccupied father ignoring his son. This unfortunate pattern is in time revisited on the father by the son, and then by the son on his son. It's a heart-wrenching downward cycle that must be broken, for the sake of every father and every son, and for the well-being of society. Breaking the cycle starts with a few caring minutes.

I have some advice for self-absorbed parents who thoughtlessly ignore their offspring and interrupt social civility with inane cell-phone conversations: turn the phone off more often, or replace it with a garage door opener.

Parrots Can't Land on Hasty Heads

Late Friday afternoon with the July 4th long weekend about to begin I was preparing to drive home when Jeff came to my office door excited about closing a large transaction with a builder. He had known about the opportunity for a couple of weeks, but that afternoon had decided my involvement would be necessary. He said the builder needed to meet on Saturday morning.

Explaining that I would have a house full of family for the weekend, I asked Jeff if we could meet later. I told him that I would make his meeting a priority after the weekend. Jeff was selfishly consistent in always making his lack of planning a problem for someone else. Although he was irritated, on my way home he called to say the builder had agreed to meet first thing on Tuesday.

On Saturday morning when I would have been meeting with the builder a neighbor, Joan Riley, called to say she had seen a colorful parrot fly from her yard to ours. A few minutes later the parrot landed on a tree branch overlooking one of our bird feeders. I grabbed a handful of peanuts and walked slowly out on the deck uttering my best version of, "Polly want a peanut?"

Andrew and Cousin Emily were ecstatic when the beautiful bird landed on my head. I carefully walked from the deck to the screened porch, where the parrot decided to hop from my head to the table for more peanuts, lettuce and a cup of cool water. Everyone was taken by the parrot's trusting friendliness. Andrew and Emily made signs to hang on poles around our small city, an effort that led to the return of the healthy bird to its grateful owner. We eschewed a reward in favor of being able to visit the parrot in the future. The feeling of accomplishment and doing the right thing was accompanied by more than a few tears as the kids said goodbye to the personable parrot. Thinking of Jeff and what I would have missed, I thankfully confirmed that parrots can't land on hasty heads.

Only Brush the Ones You Want to Keep

The best thing to give your enemy is forgiveness; to an opponent, tolerance; to a friend, your heart; to your child, a good example; to a father, deference; to your mother, conduct that will make her proud of you; to yourself, respect; to all men, charity.

- Benjamin Franklin

The anticipation of our three-day expedition to the Okefenokee National Wildlife Refuge continued to grow. Over a delicious dinner of Mandy's roasted chicken, potatoes and green beans we decided not to wait until morning. We'd pack the car that evening and leave for Waycross, Georgia.

The spontaneous change of plans only added to our excitement. At our destination was the Okefenokee Swamp Railroad, an open-air train that would transport us to the fringe of one of America's last remaining primitive wetlands. We also had high expectations for the Folkston Funnel, a multiple of tracks serving as the main artery for railroad traffic into and out of Florida. From the viewing platform in Folkston, visitors can see up to seventy-five trains per day passing to and from Jacksonville, Florida on their way north to Savannah or west to Waycross.

We packed our things, exchanged waves with Mandy, and pulled out of the driveway at about 7 pm, anticipating reaching Waycross by midnight. Our spirits lifted as we slipped Vivaldi's *Four Seasons* into the CD player and entered the Interstate express lane to another adventure.

After a rest stop for hot chocolate in Cordele, we chose the less-traveled Highway 41 and rolled the windows down. It was a brilliant starlit night, and the cool air laden with bouquets of late-summer country was most rewarding. As we continued our drive, the anticipation of seeing alligators in the swamp and of trains passing through the Folkston Funnel postponed sleep, so we decided to review some of our favorite sayings.

Andrew loves to swim, so we make every effort to find lodgings with well-maintained swimming pools. "No pool, no deal," has become one of our favorite sayings. However, after discussing this adage and reviewing some recent experiences, we decided to change it to, "no clean pool, no deal."

We also make an effort to stay within our budget. Sometimes these goals conflict, but that only helps develop our bargaining skills. We have found many innkeepers kindly sensitive to our budget limitations, and we usually do better than the posted rate.

One evening not long after Andrew started brushing his teeth without help, he asked, "Do I have to brush my teeth tonight?"

"Only the ones you want to keep," I responded, offering my son the same sage advice my father had given me. Smiling, Andrew began making a practice of regularly brushing all his teeth – and "only brush the ones you want to keep" entered our family lexicon.

"We have two ears and one mouth, and we should use them proportionately," is another family saying. So is, "never place anything smaller than your elbow in your ear."

The latter dates back to a health class Kimberly had taken in grade school. I was helping her with homework, tape-recording information from a chapter in her textbook, when she fell asleep. After carrying her to bed I continued taping, but after losing it to laughter on all occasions I finally gave up attempting to say, "Never place anything smaller than your elbow in your ear." I've often wished I'd kept that cassette.

Andrew looks right and I look left as we pass through railroad crossings. If we don't see either a train or a green light indicating that a train is on the tracks, we say, "nothing my way," and "let's stay on the highway." When we see a green light signaling an approaching locomotive, we stop in a safe place and watch the train go past. Bur first we don our headset ear muffs.

Showing respect for trains, for other people and for our hearing is consistent with our goal of being gentlemen. I think Andrew understands that our colloquial sayings are merely a fun way of learning to set standards – standards that we hope will lead to a successful life. Respect is an essential virtue for a successful life, and self-respect is the foundation of all other forms of respect.

An Alligator and a Corn Snake

It was after midnight when we reached Waycross and pulled up to a Days Inn, where the night clerk regretfully informed me that due to a convention all motels were full. I pondered our predicament in the car with my sleeping son. The excitement of shunning reservations in favor of spontaneity was gone. Our best option appeared to be spending an uncomfortable night in the car. Returning to the night window to inquire about other possibilities, the concerned clerk suggested a Super 8 Motel that catered to train engineers, not conventioneers. This advice seemed far more practical than what I had been thinking.

In my tired state I had been wondering if somewhere in town a motel might be saving a room for an impromptu visit by the President of the United States. Since most hotels only hold rooms until midnight and there was no news of the president being in Waycross that evening, perhaps we could get his room. As a sweetener, we would agree to give up the room if the president did show up, even after midnight. Or perhaps we could share it with the Commander in Chief. During my many years of travel I'd heard stories of certain hotels saving rooms for the president and other dignitaries, but unfortunately I couldn't recall the president staying at a Super 8.

Driving over to the Super 8, Andrew woke up. I explained our dilemma, and we began praying for a favorable outcome. We entered the lobby with a sense of anticipation.

"Yes," said the woman behind the counter. "We have one room left!"

We paid with none of our usual haggling and gratefully retrieved our bag from the car. The next morning I ran a bath for Andrew. Looking at the full bathtub and imagining a swimming pool with depth markings, he asked, "Where are the numbers?"

Our fortuitous Super 8 stay was further rewarded when we came across three CSX train engineers talking shop over coffee. As we listened, I watched Andrew's interest grow.

Anticipating a good reception, I introduced my son as a train buff. Sure enough, the engineers made time to talk to their enthusiastic admirer. They recommended that we visit the CSX repair yard in Waycross, where we would see the latest and most powerful GE locomotive. We agreed to do so on our way home. Thanking them for their hospitality, we made our way to the north entrance of the fascinating Okefenokee Swamp.

Covering approximately 700 square miles of South Georgia and North Florida, the Okefenokee Swamp is a bowl-shaped depression twenty-five miles across and forty miles long. A unique primitive wetland and national treasure, the Okefenokee is comprised of a variety of habitats harboring hundreds of birds, mammals, reptiles and amphibians, many of which are endangered or threatened. Plant life in the Okefenokee varies from towering bald cypress to an almost infinite variety of water plants.

The north end of the swamp is bordered by pine forests and thick tangles of vegetation. Small water trails lead south to the open prairies and west to the Suwannee River. Nearly 400,000 acres of this land were designated as the Okefenokee National Wildlife Refuge in 1937, protecting the headwaters of the Suwannee and St. Mary's Rivers from further human development. Both rivers are now among the most beautiful watersheds in the southeastern United States and carry clean, nutrient-rich water across the coastal plain to the sea.

Andrew was most excited about the train ride into the swamp. The Okefenokee Swamp Railroad features the diesel-powered Lady Suwannee, a replica of a steam engine, which pulls four cars along a one-and-a-half-mile loop. On the open-air train we did indeed see an alligator, and when we stopped at Pioneer Island we discovered a country store complete with chocolate ice cream.

The island's treasures included an historic home complete with outhouse. I found it fascinating trying to explain the workings of an outhouse to my five-year-old. I am always amazed at how many things I thought I understood, but have difficulty explaining to my child.

After a boat ride on the dark and mysterious waters of the Okefenokee, we visited the wildlife center and met an American Indian. The Creek Indian told a small group of parents and children about the swamp and its many creatures. When he offered to let them touch a baby alligator and a couple of beautiful snakes, the other children pulled back but Andrew bravely accepted. The American Indian (a name he preferred over Native American) asked us to stay after the show, and allowed my enthralled son to hold a two-foot-long orange

Corn Snake. It was a fitting end to our day exploring the treasures of the Okefenokee.

Finding Favor

That night watching one of our favorite movies, *Trains, Planes, and Automobiles,* (a family-friendly version) with John Candy and Steve Martin, Andrew fell asleep and I took the opportunity for a quiet moment of reflection. My recent re-reading of *Miracles* by C.S. Lewis, one of the world's most-quoted and respected authors, influenced my thinking.

I want Andrew to believe in miracles and to expect them in his life. I know he has found favor with God, and that will continue. But what mysterious forces had intervened last night on our behalf? How had we found the only room available in Waycross? And how did it happen that our room was in a motel catering to train engineers?

Finding the room may not have been a miracle. But it was surely a special occurrence, and confirmation that God rewards those who seek His favor.

The Fabulous Funnel

The best of a person's life may very well be seemingly small acts of kindness shown daily.
                                        - Anonymous

We had high expectations for the Folkston Funnel, and we were not disappointed. The good people of Folkston have built a viewing platform complete with speakers. Watching train after train traveling north and south, meeting and passing one another right before our wide eyes, listening through the speakers to dispatchers communicating with engineers, it was almost like being inside the trains.

As I've mentioned, train people are generally affable and good-hearted, but in Folkston we saw some who went above and beyond. These veterans know where the faithful will be, such as at crossings near children's parks, and as they approach these areas they lean out the window with a wide wave, a broad smile and a customized toot of the whistle. These engineers joyfully cross over the line, from merely working at a job to being ambassadors of an era.

The thrill of an approaching train energizes both young and old, and with seventy-five trains roaring through Folkston daily there is no shortage of available energy. Watching tons of rolling iron grandly and dutifully carrying people and goods to places near and far, feeling my son's tireless excitement, I too waved at every passing train. His wonderful intensity is inspiring. Once again, I savored my good fortune in being able to share adventures like this with him.

Twice that day we visited the Folkston platform. On the second occasion a father-and-son team was filming the trains with lots of expensive camera equipment. They, too, were enjoying one another's company, but they weren't waving to the engineers. It occurred to me that maybe they were missing out because they were "too old" to be waving at trains.

I realize that many people would consider my waving at trains odd, with or without Andrew. But as the Popeye of my childhood so aptly said, "I knows what I like." I think it should give us pause when we don't encourage boys to be boys, when we feel too old to allow the boy within us to emerge.

There is a time and a place for maturity and responsibility, and there is a time and a place for boyish fun. A boy will become a better man, and a man a better father, husband and friend, when he nurtures his boyish spirit. The vulnerability in reaching out toward life makes us more interesting people.

Noble Stillness

On the last day of our three-day excursion, Andrew and I re-entered the Okefenokee Swamp at the Folkston entrance. Native Americans call this the "land of trembling earth." It looked virtually the same as it had some fifty years before when I had first visited the magnificent refuge with my parents and siblings.

The Folkston entrance is even more primitive and natural than the entrance at Waycross. It is a timeless sanctuary from our ever-diminishing forests, plants and creatures. The swirl of a fish in ebony water, stately Cypress trees adorned with Spanish moss, the bright colors of wildflowers, all combine to form a noble, immense stillness.

For a father and son, it is a wonderful place for reverent contemplation. For a long time Andrew and I sat placidly in a small boat, meditatively listening to the sounds of the swamp, thankful for our shared solitude.

Chapter Ten

REUNION

*It's frightening to think that you mark your child
merely by being yourself.*

- Simone de Beauvoir

According to the calendar, summer passed the baton to autumn on September 23 but our warm, sunny days continued unabated. Mandy and I were discussing an upcoming reunion for the associates of First Federal of Miami. Spouses were invited but few had registered, and Mandy suggested that Andrew accompany me instead.

First Federal, my first full-time employer right out of college, had the distinction of being the first federally chartered savings and loan in America. It was the largest federal S&L in Florida when it was purchased in the late eighties. Owned by the people who had accounts with the institution, the bank was committed to fostering the American dream of home ownership.

Those of us who worked there in the seventies were thankful for the opportunity. Then people were more likely to see home ownership as a privilege. They worked hard and saved up enough money for a meaningful down payment, then they qualified for a loan within their means.

That was the way it was supposed to work, but somehow over the years home ownership became a right. Mortgage loans, including government-sponsored Federal Housing Administration (FHA) loans, became available to qualifying people at ever-higher ratios. Delinquencies and foreclosures followed accordingly and have now risen to crisis levels. The same federal government that for years badgered lenders to offer mortgage loans to unqualified borrowers is now looking for a scapegoat everywhere but in the mirror. The government wants to blame someone else for the harm it has done to a multitude of families, and to our country. Those who insisted that tried and proven lending standards be lowered or tossed have hurt the very people they ostensibly sought to help. We continue to elect officials who think that somehow we can hand over a right without a related responsibility. Politicians are like permissive parents – more concerned about being liked than about doing what is right. Yet we cannot absolve bankers from their culpability – most were eager to initiate marginal loans as long as they made money in the process. Free lunches almost always taste bitter. I liked it better when home ownership required that you work and save.

First Federal of Miami was founded by William Walker, and after his death it was managed by his sons and then his grandchildren. It was a great place to work and I made lasting friendships that continue to enrich my life. At the first reunion a few years ago we had a good turnout of more than a hundred former employees.

For most of us, many years had passed since we had seen one another. We all enjoyed a rewarding experience with much reminiscing and laughter and many tall tales. Time had taken its toll on everyone, although some less than others. The invincibility we had felt in the early years of our careers had been replaced by the sobering reality that we were not bigger than life. This was most apparent when we observed a moment of prayerful silence for those whose lives had been claimed by war, accidents and disease.

The first reunion had been held in Coconut Grove at the Chart House restaurant overlooking beautiful Biscayne Bay, and it had brought back fond memories for many of us who had fished, sailed and played on Miami's waterways. Bob Lydzinski dryly observed that much of the hair receding from the heads of the men had apparently fallen, and was now thriving in their ears.

The most rewarding aspect of that first reunion was being with friends. He who laughs best is probably doing so with friends. Memories about the first reunion heightened my expectations for the second, and at Mandy's urging I decided to measure Andrew's interest in joining me. First Federal had been a major chapter in my life, and I would enjoy sharing the memories with my son.

I hadn't yet asked the organizers of the reunion if Andrew could attend, and I didn't want to talk to Andrew about the reunion until I had an answer, but I could measure his interest by talking about growing up in Florida. I began to focus our bedtime stories on my childhood in Miami.

I shared memories of growing up in a pastoral Florida where dairy farms, Seminole Indian villages and coconut palms were more common than mega-subdivisions. Andrew had already been though a couple of cold winters at Berkeley Lake – one year we even had enough snow to slide down the incline of our driveway on trash can lids – so my stories about walking along South Florida beaches on Christmas Day, and even swimming in the ocean, were fascinating to him.

South Florida has four seasons – summer, summer, summer and a short spring – with one notable exception. Many years ago I was on my way to work at our new First Federal of Miami branch, our first in Palm Beach County, where I was the proud manager. Waiting at a railroad crossing in Boca Raton, listening to Alabama's song *Christmas in Dixie* on the radio as the train rumbled by, I looked at the car beside mine and experienced a pleasant surprise. Falling snow was melting on the car's warm hood.

In the forty years I lived in Florida that was the only snow I ever witnessed. When I arrived at work, one of the tellers, Pat Tracey, was at the door smiling. She asked for the day off to go home and play in the snow with her daughter, Tiffany. I somewhat reticently obliged. Pat and her husband Jack were hard working people who nonetheless knew it was important to make time for family. Today, Pat owns her own successful company and Tiffany is an accomplished medical doctor. I'm glad they were able to share that day in the snow years before. Andrew also thought it was a great idea.

I told Andrew that after being with First Federal of Miami for twelve years it was with some trepidation that I resigned my position in 1983. I was starting a new job closer to home that required less travel and let me spend more time with Dawn and Kimberly. I made the right decision to spend more time with my daughters, but I did miss working with the people at First Federal.

Mostly I missed my relationship with Tom Bomar. Tom was my mentor and later he was my friend. Tom was the first non-Walker to hold the positions of president and chairman of First Federal. Andrew and I talked about my gratitude and admiration for Tom, and about the significance of having quality mentors in our lives. Tom had a storied career. His confidence and encouragement motivated me and many others to stretch for more lofty goals. When Tom brought Joe Reppert in to become president of the S & L's mortgage company, I worked for Joe in some areas and for Tom in others.

Joe tells a story about Ed Neff, one of my peers, requesting a meeting with Tom and Joe to ask for my scalp. Ed pointed out that I was always rocking the boat. He suggested that my habit of challenging procedures and authority was counter-productive. Joe deferred to Tom and sat silently as Ed outlined his complaints. Tom agreed that I had a tendency to question things, but said, "Every successful company needs someone to question the status quo. Nick's our boat rocker."

Ed never brought the subject up again. He was one of the people for whom we had shared a moment of prayer at the first reunion. If he had lived long enough to attend, I'm sure he and I would have had some good laughs about that incident. Time and maturity usually help us get past our egos and our jockeying for status. Being secure in who we are provides a therapeutic ability to forgive, and to laugh at ourselves.

After a few nights of stories, I knew Andrew was interested in joining me at the second reunion. He already liked Tom for saving his dad's job. Walt Kabis, the organizer, asked if I would be Master of Ceremonies for the luncheon. I readily agreed, with the caveat that Andrew be allowed to attend as my guest. Walt cautioned that there would be no other children, but he agreed to let Andrew come.

Andrew and I talked about the importance of being on his best behavior. Neither of us were concerned that there would be no other children in attendance. Andrew wanted to meet my friends and former associates, and I wanted him to be there.

Memories and Exploits

I looked over my son's head at the planes, trains and automobiles becoming smaller as our Delta flight lifted off from busy Harts-field-Jackson International Airport. Rising through gray mist we managed a brief look at Atlanta's skyline before the Boeing banked right and proceeded south to Ft. Lauderdale. Andrew's attention was soon drawn to a multitude of white clouds.

"Daddy, can we walk on clouds?" he asked.

After discussing how much fun it would be to run across the sky hopping from one balmy white pillow to the next, agreeing that it would be even more fun to do it with friends, Andrew fell silent and was soon deep in slumber. An hour into our flight the jet banked and began gliding effortlessly back toward the ocean. Andrew woke and watched the wondrous Florida Everglades rising up to meet us. I confirmed that the everglades are indeed much like Georgia's Okefenokee Swamp.

We were having dinner with my nephew Steven, Andrew's cousin, at Carlos and Pepe's, a popular restaurant on the 17 Street causeway in Ft. Lauderdale and an easy drive from the airport. It was great to observe a thirty-something and a five-year-old conversing. Andrew shared his disappointment that Steven's girlfriend had not come. Agreeing that she should have chosen to miss her college class, we teasingly suggested that Steven might want to rethink the relationship. Steven, in turn, told Andrew stories about how Uncle Nick had played pranks on him and Brian, his brother.

Steven also told Andrew about the time his other uncle Jimmy had rented a tux and a shiny black stretch limo for me. Only a few days home after completing my four-year military obligation, little did I know that my first job out of the Air Force would be as a movie star.

The tux and limo were props. The movie *Tony Roma* starring Frank Sinatra and Jill St. John was being filmed on the bay in Miami. Jimmy, my ever-creative and multi-talented brother-in-law's brother, had written a song. I was to get the song into Sinatra's hands by impersonating a movie star.

The limo was met by a throng of shrieking young woman. They had no idea who I was, and at that point neither did I, but a young man arriving by limo in a smart tux must be somebody. With mixed emotions of elation and fear, and with Jimmy watching from above on the 79 Street causeway bridge, I left the safety of the stretch sedan and easily gained access to a large, crowded tent.

The crew was celebrating Jill St. John's birthday. After a few minutes I spotted Mr. Sinatra sitting in a director's chair. Anxiously I sat next him. When he asked my name, I nervously handed him Jimmy's creation. Looking on from a safe distance, Jimmy flipped out as Mr. Sinatra good-naturedly accepted the music. I thanked him, shook his hand and excused myself in one fluid motion. Making haste back to the waiting limo through the still-shrieking throng of fans, I no longer felt counterfeit – now they were fussing over the guy who had just shaken Frank Sinatra's hand.

Mission accomplished, my brief movie-star status ended abruptly. It still seems like only yesterday. Andrew was much amused by Steven's story, although he would have been even more impressed if I'd delivered something to the *Naked Brothers Band*. But anyone older than five may have heard *Strangers in the Night* a few times. It was handed to Mr. Sinatra by a stranger.

Restless Hearts

Thou hast made us for Thyself O God, and our hearts are restless 'til they find their rest in thee.

- Saint Augustine

Andrew and I drove north along the ocean toward our lodgings only one short block from legendary Ft. Lauderdale Beach. In our room we had an unanticipated yet much-appreciated sliver of an ocean view, and the pool was even closer than the ocean.

"Andrew, how fortunate are we?" I asked.

"Very. Can we go to the beach now?"

We changed into beachwear and were soon under a rising moon

experiencing the always-wonderful feeling of sand between our toes. Walking in the surf, we headed toward the Angling Pier area of Lauderdale by the Sea, a place that had meant a great deal to me in my own childhood. I loved sharing the roar of the surf and the spray with Andrew, and his reaction was an energized, "Awesome!"

Confirming that the funky Pier Restaurant was still serving breakfast outdoors, we walked along the venerable pier still dotted with faithful fisherman also enjoying the evening trade winds. For many fishermen the unspoken sentiment is, "If we catch something, great – but time on the ocean is its own reward."

Quickening our pace, we watched a man reel in a large crab clutching a piece of bait. The crustacean found himself in a dilemma not unlike the human experience. Uncomprehendingly holding his prize, pondering the meaning of his ascent, knowing he should let go, desire ruled over reason. Without warning, the crab was knocked from his precarious perch into the unknown and gone was his prize, along with everything else that had meaning to him.

Andrew and I found an empty pier bench and shared a quiet moment. The sea has no equal in providing tranquility, and tonight with the moon deliberately and marvelously climbing up the horizon it was exceptional. Very little in our earthly experience is at the same time as awesome and as tranquil as the moon rising out of the sea. Watching two of the Maker's most extraordinary creations, a kaleidoscope of magnificence rising triumphantly above a tumultuous, multicolored ocean, I told my attentive son there is a great longing in every person, and that longing can only be satisfied by the Creator. It may have been too much for him to understand, but the moment was right.

The Greatest of Worldly Goods

Friendship is the greatest of worldly goods. Certainly to me it

*is the chief happiness of life. If I had to give a piece of advice
to a young man about where to live, I think I should say,
"sacrifice almost everything to live where you can be near your
friends."*

- *C.S. Lewis*

Andrew and I drove to the Hard Rock resort and entered the reunion luncheon to effusive greetings, hand-shaking and hugging.
Earlier in the day I had prepped him with a few facts that would
get him though most of the questions. He knew he would likely
be asked his age and level of matriculation, and he was prepared
to clearly respond.

Sitting at a table of eight, Andrew was on his best behavior. Hon-
oring his dad's advice, he offered a firm handshake with good eye
contact, and clearly spoke his name. He remembered that he had
just turned five, and that he was attending Pleasant Hill Pre-school
three days a week. He knew he lived on Berkeley Lake in Georgia
with his mom and dad, Mandy and Nick Lore. He also related that
he was allergic to oatmeal.

Bob and Dorothy Lydzinski and others at the table made him feel
welcome. Bob and I have been friends for more than thirty years,
and Bob's great sense of humor provided much amusement for Andrew as he embellished many tales about my career. Andrew was
most interested in hearing how some two dozens years ago Bob and

I had made the Halloween morning traffic report.
I was driving my Buick along the Interstate 95 carpool lane wearing a gorilla costume, with Bob beside me in pirate's guise. Happily waving to a mixed crowd of amused and angry commuters,
we turned on the radio.

"Traffic is slowing just before 79 Street going into downtown," we
heard the announcer saying. "People are looking at a couple of nuts
dressed up for Halloween."

That was the last radio traffic report Bob and I heard before an angry Florida highway patrolman invited us off the Interstate. Chiding us for slowing traffic, he also issued me an illustration of his displeasure on paper.

Andrew asked me to repeat the story later that night. Warning him never to copy my stunt, I told Andrew it was memorable but not one of our better ideas. Andrew acknowledged my caveat, but I was nevertheless glad that since that long-ago time, my actions have spoken louder than my words.

My friends Bob Lydzinski, Walt Kabis, Gail Koptowsky and Marti Bullman were among the many folks who made a five-year-old feel welcome at a reunion luncheon. They confirmed that friendships are a form of great joy. I'm fortunate in that respect, and happy that Andrew is eager to further develop his own growing circle of friends. I was also pleased when he told me that at the reunion he learned it is possible to be on your best behavior and still have fun.

Observing the Incomprehensible

Just remember this, my girl, when you look up in the sky
You can see the stars and still not see the light

- Eagles; Already Gone lyrics

Our top-floor hotel room offered no loss of privacy with the curtains open, so we woke with the rising sun. Brushing only the ones we wanted to keep, we dressed for the beach. In my mind Saturday morning has always been synonymous with friends, adventure and carefree fun – what better place to be on a Saturday morning than at the beach?

Crossing the quiet road separating the hotel from the Atlantic, we were courteously stopped by a Broward County sheriff's deputy who warned of serious rip tides in the ocean. Thanking him for his concern, we agreed to stay close to shore. Settling on the beach to watch the sun rise, Andrew was awash with questions about rip tides.

Walking barefoot back to Angling Pier, we arrived at the Pier Restaurant early enough to have only a short wait for an outdoor ocean-side table. Sharing breakfast with a full view of the ocean, we watched a spectacular sunrise turning cumulus clouds into a brilliant array of colors.

Observing the diners inside the air-conditioned restaurant engrossed in conversation and oblivious to the magnificent spectacle unfolding outside, I said to Andrew, "All of us are watchers – of television, of time clocks, of traffic on the freeway – but few of us are observers. Everyone is looking, but not many are seeing."

So much of what Andrew and I share together involves observing the Creator's natural artistry. In nature we experience so much of what we pray for, so much of what we hope that our souls will forever experience. In nature, we come as close as we can get to understanding eternity.

I told my son that some people don't want to believe in a God they don't completely comprehend. I believe that on this side of heaven a being who I can fully understand is not big enough to be God. In our brief, earthly sojourn, we are not equipped to fully understand the Almighty. God is incomprehensible because we must approach Him as He intended; in faith.

Being Our Best

Back on shore I told Andrew that somewhere in the sand were the footprints of many taxing practice runs I had taken with my high school teammates Alex Czipulis, Gary Hight, Fred Taub and Archie Turner. We encouraged one another and ran through the pain with the goal of being our best.

As Andrew prodded for more information, we talked about commitment and winning. I told him my teammates and I ran on the shore from Hallover Beach in Miami along Hollywood and Ft. Lauderdale beaches to as far north as Boca Raton. Running long and hard, we built enduring bonds between us. We also built strong character that thrived in hard work and adversity. Sharing our aspirations and dreams, we paid the price because we knew that was what it took to be our best, perhaps even to be champions. The special joy and camaraderie we shared had meaning beyond our desire to win. Somewhere deep within us, we knew these special times were being etched onto our rising spirits.

In our senior year we realized our dream. We celebrated what was then the fastest high school mile relay race ever run in the state of Florida.

Andrew wanted to know if he, too, would have buddies and be a winning athlete. I assured him that his friendships would continue to grow, and that by being his best he would indeed be a champion.

I Hope You Dance

I hope you still feel small when you stand by the ocean
- Lee Ann Womack,
(I Hope You Dance lyrics)

Finally yielding to temptation, we ventured cautiously into the water. The strong rip tide tugged us out to sea, but we resisted its primal pull. I believe men of all ages have an innate desire to dance with danger. So much of what we do confirms that excitement and danger are fruits of the same tree. Just ask Adam.

In late morning we decided to heed the officer's advice. Even at thigh depth, the unceasing tugging of the waves was tiring. Leaving behind the turbulent surf, we sat watching a group of young surfers reveling in the blustery waves. Wishing them a tenacious ten for safe passage to shore, I heard the question even before it was spoken.

"Daddy, when can I go surfing?"

Building castles is great fun. When Andrew was younger, we erected our first structures without concern for the direction of the tide or proximity to the surf, then haplessly watched as our construction projects disappeared into the unforgiving ocean. As we learned to plan better, our gritty mansions gained in stature and durability. That day in Ft. Lauderdale, our castle was nothing less than a masterpiece.

After admiring the fruits of our labor sparkling in the early afternoon sun, we hoofed it back to the hotel swimming pool. I asked Andrew what he would like for lunch.

"Daddy, let's just have a root beer and chat," he said.
It's a fortunate father whose son cares to chat with him. Rightfully so, most families keep photographs of their little darlings. I also enjoy writing conversational keepsakes in my journal. Importantly to my mind, conversation includes the creative art of empathic listening. It should not be mistaken for mere talk. I'm beginning to understand that listening is a valuable teaching tool. Too often, I've spoken when I should have listened. I have many recollections of getting into trouble for what I have said, but far fewer for being silent.

Our kids need to be heard. I am humbled by the joy Andrew feels knowing that I am listening to him. Ordering a couple of root beers, we found a table by the pool. As Andrew chatted and I listened, Lee Ann Womack's song *I Hope You Dance* began playing on the poolside stereo. Perhaps it was mere chance, but I chose to believe it was more than that.

I Hope You Dance

> I hope you never lose your sense of wonder
> You get your fill to eat

But always keep that hunger
May you never take one single breath for granted
God forbid love ever leave you empty handed

I hope you still feel small
When you stand by the ocean

Whenever one door closes, I hope one more opens
Promise me you'll give faith a fighting chance

And when you get the choice to sit it out or dance
I hope you dance
I hope you dance

I hope you never fear those mountains in the distance
Never settle for the path of least resistance
Living might mean taking chances
But they're worth taking
Lovin' might be a mistake
But it's worth making
Don't let some hell bent heart
Leave you bitter
When you come close to selling out
Reconsider
Give the heavens above
More than just a passing glance

And when you get the choice to sit it out or dance
I hope you dance
(Time is a real and constant motion always)
I hope you dance
(Rolling us along)
I hope you dance
(Tell me who)
I hope you dance
(Wants to look back on their youth and wonder)

(Where those years have gone)

I hope you still feel small

When you stand by the ocean
Whenever one door closes, I hope one more opens
Promise me you'll give faith a fighting chance

And when you get the choice to sit it out or dance
Dance
I hope you dance
I hope you dance
(Time is a real and constant motion always)
I hope you dance
(Rolling us along)
I hope you dance

(Tell me who)
(Wants to look back on their youth and wonder)
I hope you dance
(Where those years have gone)
(Tell me who)
I hope you dance
(Wants to look back on their youth and wonder)
(Where those years have gone)

- Lee Ann Womack

Chapter Eleven

PERFECTLY FLAWED

*Courage is rightly esteemed the first of human qualities because
it is the quality which guarantees all others.*

- Winston Churchill

Sipping hot tea, I watched a beautiful light rain dancing on the lake.
There was time to let Andrew sleep a little longer. It was the first
day of December, a day we had long anticipated. Soon we would be
on our way to Chattanooga, where the Tennessee Valley Railroad's
North Pole Limited would take us to visit Santa Claus.

When Andrew woke we sat in our bedroom recliner, where we have
shared so many books and stories. Listening to the rain on our roof
reminded me of a story about the perfectly flawed aprons.

I was nine years old. Mom and I were driving back home in heavy
rain after my first meeting with Mrs. Lazarus. The windshield wip-
ers on our 1953 Pontiac were flapping rapidly, and on the car's bench
seat were six handmade aprons.

Mom explained what Aunt Jenny had told her. Mrs. Lazarus had lost her entire family to the Nazis. After moving to the United States, she now lived alone a few doors down from my Aunt Jenny in a modest South Miami apartment. Mrs. Lazarus lived on some sort of small disability pension from Germany and the proceeds from her cheerful red and white hand-sewn aprons, which she sold in a consignment shop for fifty cents each. I had a cursory understanding of World War II, but I had never before met someone so affected by the abject evil of Nazi Germany.

Mom and Aunt Jenny had been pitching my services as a salesman to Mrs. Lazarus. Mom once said that I could sell ice to Eskimos, and Aunt Jenny had told Mrs. Lazarus that her ambitious nephew was a natural-born salesman. Holding up one of her aprons, Mrs. Lazarus proposed that we split the fifty cents evenly.

This seemed fair to me – it would supplement my other incomes from cutting grass and selling stuff, but Mom had a different thought. She suggested a more equitable split would be thirty-five cents for Mrs. Lazarus and fifteen cents for me. The larger share for Mrs. Lazarus would cover the cost of her materials and her time in making the garment. Mom pointed out that it shouldn't take long for "a salesman of your ability" to peddle the aprons.

Dad helped me practice my sales pitch. I had never sold aprons, but I'd built a strong customer base mowing lawns and selling TV Guides and tomatoes. My customers were good folks, but I knew they would only buy if they wanted what I was selling. It would be a true test for my proposed venture with Mrs. Lazarus. Riding my bike to the affluent neighborhood where my customers lived, my heart raced with anticipation as I knocked on the first door.

"Paul, give me twenty-five cents – it's the tomato boy!" said the lady who answered.

Andrew smiled broadly, tickled at the thought of his dad being the tomato boy, in his vivid imagination seeing a plump red nine-year-old standing on the porch.

"Don't you usually come on Saturday mornings?" Mrs. Rogers asked. Flustered and wishing I had brought my tomatoes, I recovered and launched into my Friday-afternoon pitch.

"Yes, but today I'm selling this beautiful handmade apron sewn by a lady from Germany."

Looking over the checkered garment, Mrs. Rogers noted that one tie was longer than the other. She said she thought the price was high.

The Rogers used the same scrutiny when I cut their grass. The first time I mowed and edged the Rogers' lawn they had wanted it just right, and they about drove me crazy, but eventually the lawn was acceptable and I was better for it. The Rogers became loyal clients for lots of things and a good source of referrals. The Rogers taught me the value of a job well done. They also taught me the value of preparation. I always felt that they enjoyed the banter, regardless of what I was selling.

Fortunately, my dad had prepared me for the "imperfect" objection.

"All of the aprons are uniquely different," I said. "That is what makes them special."

"But why doesn't she stick to the pattern?" Mrs. Rogers countered.

Neither Dad nor anyone else had covered this objection. I was on my own. Revealing the reason would risk betraying Mrs. Lazarus. Would mentioning it be wrong? Would it make her sewing less appreciated? It wasn't part of my prepared script and I hadn't planned ahead, but it seemed appropriate to inform Mrs. Rogers that the reason Mrs. Lazarus couldn't stick to the pattern was that she was blind.

A sharp intake of breath informed me that Andrew had understood.

He was inspired by how a blind woman could sew.

"People are like aprons," I told him. "Our differences and our imperfections make us special."

Excited about selling my first apron and emboldened, I decided I'd make fifty sales calls that day. On the forty-seventh call, I sold my last apron. Elated, I rode my bike home in near-darkness and called Aunt Jenny and Mrs. Lazarus. I had missed dinner with my family but they, too, were euphoric over the sale of my six perfectly flawed aprons.

The following week Mrs. Lazarus provided six more aprons. In short order I was selling twelve garments a week. After selling sixty aprons between Thanksgiving and Christmas, we celebrated with Sunday dinner at Aunt Jenny's apartment. Offering the blessing, Mrs. Lazarus thanked God for her new family.

Who You Marry

Andrew was all smiles as I finished my story. Wanting to leave him with a moral lesson, I thought about the role of Aunt Jenny and my mom, both of whom had believed in me and who had assured Mrs. Lazarus of my commitment and determination. My strong desire to meet the expectations of these women had played a huge role in my success.

"Andrew, this story is about the wonderful motivation that women can bring to your life. The influence of good women, especially your mother and your wife, will inspire you to great heights."

"Dad, tell me again about if I marry," he answered.

"Who you marry is one of the most important decisions you will make, second only to loving God." I said. "God has plans for your life, and who you marry will affect His plans for you."

We paused to watch the rain falling on our lake.

"Remember to choose your friends wisely. This is especially important for the person who should be your best friend, your wife. You must take meaningful time to make a great decision. The woman you share your life with will significantly affect everything else, including your spiritual, physical and intellectual well-being."

I closed the apron story knowing there would be another opportunity to retell it, and other life lessons to revisit. Now we needed to get going.

Bad Guys Finish Last

Just because you're afraid doesn't mean you aren't brave.
Being brave means doing what you have to do no matter how
scared you feel.
> *- Paulette Bourgeois and Brenda Clark*
> *(Franklin Goes to the Hospital)*

Wearing our Sunday best, we drove to Berkeley Lake Elementary School for our Christmas lunch date with Mandy. Lunch was festive, with the school choir singing carols against the high-pitched background roar of excited children. Our friends and neighbors Phil and Beth Gilbert arrived shortly after we sat down. We chatted and ate, and when Mandy returned to her class Andrew and I retrieved our soggy umbrella and bid everyone adieu.

The school where Mandy teaches is only a mile from our house. After returning home to change into jeans, our plan was to drive to Chattanooga for the train ride to visit Santa. Driving home, Andrew said that a boy in his pre-school class had told him there is no Santa. I replied that St. Nicholas is real to all who have joyful hearts. The rain had picked up, so we parked in our driveway and postponed the task of taking the trash container in the garage up to the curb. Entering our house, Andrew suddenly stopped.

"Daddy, why is the porch screen on the kitchen table?"

Had Mandy left the screen there? But that was impossible – we had eaten breakfast at that table after she left for work. My mind raced to find an answer. After spending precious moments trying to understand the situation, it clicked.

"Andrew, get out of the house now!"

In an emergency, Andrew was to run toward the side door and his safe hiding place. At that moment two thugs who had been burglarizing our bedroom came thundering down the stairs. One ran out the front door, but the second turned toward the side door. I glanced at Andrew, and a large knife on the counter caught my attention. My heart pounding, I braced myself and hit the burglar hard with a forearm across his chest. It felt unlike anything I'd done since playing Air Force football. Exhaling loudly, he staggered back toward the front foyer.

The crook was motivated to save his skin, while I was driven to protect my son. I had the higher calling. Fear and anger combined with a forceful shove sent him reeling out the front door, where he somehow kept his feet and raced up our driveway to rejoin his accomplice.

I turned back to find Andrew concealed in his safe hiding place. Clutching him and praising him for his prompt and valiant act, we jumped in the Marquis. Backing out of the driveway, I fumbled to dial 911.

Explaining to the 911 operator what had happened, we made a two-minute drive around the neighborhood seeking the getaway car, then circled back to our home to await the police. Bill Dixon, a neighbor, came over to say that while we were gone the bad guys had escaped. Incredibly, they had parked their car in our garage! When the police arrived, Bill and Andrew helped me explain what had transpired.

"Was anything said between you and the burglars?" the officer asked. I told him that I had yelled at them to get out of our house. Andrew interrupted me.

"Dad, can I tell you a secret?"

The officer asked that I listen to Andrew. He said children are often better witnesses than adults.

"Daddy, you didn't just say 'get out of our house.' You said, 'Get the hell out of our house you ash!'"

In laughter we found relief, but at the same time the questions came flooding in. What if we had not left the driveway to find the getaway car? What would have happened if the rain had not picked up when we arrived home? What if I'd opened the garage door to take out the trash? What if Andrew had run upstairs while I was taking out the trash? Of all my post-trauma thoughts, the latter was the most disconcerting.

Gwinnett County police officer Seymour spent two hours completing the break-in report while his associate fingerprinted suspected items. With the officers there, we began to feel comfortable again in our home. We were most fortunate that Andrew and I were okay, and we could easily repair the damage.

I chose not to call Mandy while the police were there. I didn't want her to see the utter disarray of recklessly emptied drawers and closets. It was a distressing feeling. When the police departed I left a message asking her to come directly home after school.

Everything was indeed okay. As Andrew and I talked, we agreed to be grateful for the good things that had happened that morning. I hugged him and praised him for listening, and for acting so courageously. We thanked God for keeping us safe, and for the limited damage to our home. What had been taken could be replaced. When we finished praying, my son said, "Daddy, you forgot something."

Puzzled, I inquired as to what I forgot.

"You forgot to pray for the bad guys."

I have a confession. My own reaction to the events of that day was not entirely consistent with that of my wise young son. Still unsure, I asked him precisely how we should pray for the bad guys.

"Can we pray they get jobs so they don't have to break into houses?"

While I admired my son's request, I wanted the jobs to come after they had spent a significant stint in the pokey. But children are often more forgiving than adults. I suspect that I was the less sincere, but we did offer Andrew's additional prayer.

The Key to Life

We must travel in the direction of our fear.

- John Berryman

For weeks after the break-in every bump in the night became a cause for concern, and for months Andrew was uncomfortable sleeping alone in his bedroom. Shaken by the event, we began sharing the fear and suspicion that consumes a thief's desperate existence.

The thieves had committed a felony by ransacking our home and they had risked harming us, but we needed to move forward. Mandy and I told Andrew that they had left behind an emotional stench from which we needed to free ourselves.

I once had a revealing conversation with a man who spent three years in prison for burglary, and who said prison helped turn his life around. Before prison, he was empty of love and filled with distrust.

"I didn't understand why, but I was always angry," he said. "I couldn't sleep or even rest. When the doorbell or phone rang, I worried that it was the police."

Andrew asked what happened to the man, and was surprised to discover that he was now a family friend.

"Crooks are foolish." I said. "If they'd put as much effort into honest work, they'd likely be successful."

Determined to make the break-in a positive learning experience, I reaffirmed to my maturing son that living well and respecting others is its own reward. We also affirmed that life is a series of events or seasons, some of which we can control, and some which we cannot. Some are good, and some appear to be bad. Regardless of our circumstances, the key to life is found by living each day to the fullest.

In retrospect, it was apparent that the two thugs were primarily interested in stealing our classic Ford Mustang. Rummaging desperately through our home, they had cast aside many other valuables in their hunt for the key to the car. I'm just relieved that in their feverish foray through our lives they didn't look under the driver's-side floor mat of the Mustang.

Hope Children's Home

Many years ago I decided to do something about the growing disdain I felt over the commercialization of Christmas. I decided to recapture the original spirit of the holiday, to again find peace in Christmas.

The very first Christmas gifts were few, and they were for the Child. What the observance had become, however, was distracting. More than anything, it made me feel tired. I dreaded what Christmas had become.

At first, my idea appeared radical. From now on, I would only buy gifts for my parents, for the little ones in our family, and for the less fortunate. The first two were easy, but I contemplated how to handle the others.

A few weeks after my decision, as I was still contemplating how to go about implementing my idea, a group of children came to our church to sing Christmas music. The choral group from a children's home, they were all sizes and colors and they sang wonderfully well.

Hope Ministries provided them a loving home, schooling and a place to worship on a then-modest campus in Tampa, Florida. Prior to landing in Hope Children's Home, the youngsters had experienced heartbreaking abuse and abandonment. As they sang, Scripture came to mind. Christmas was once about the birth of the Christ-child. The verse that came to mind was spoken by Him in the Gospel of Matthew:

> *Assuredly I say to you, inasmuch as you did it to one of the least of these My brethren, you did it to Me.*
> *- Matthew 25:40*

Inspired, I needed no more time to contemplate my gift-giving. That night I wrote everyone on my gift list a letter describing my new approach. The letter was straightforward. Going forward, it said, my Christmas giving to siblings, family and friends would be in the form of a donation to Hope Children's Home. I'd give an amount equal to what I customarily spent at the malls. I asked my correspondents to reciprocate, and I felt the weight of wild consumerism lifting from my shoulders.

Some of those who received the letter were relieved that they would no longer have to endure my poor gift choices. Others thought I'd lost my mind, or joined a cult. But today my crazy idea has become a family tradition that has spread beyond our family to a number of friends. A recent count included fourteen families who now make joyful annual investments in the future of children.

Ben Stein

I grew up in a modest home with few gifts but lots of love. Love brought less focus on self, and more interest in others. I remember wishing my friends – Jews and Christians alike – Merry Christmas. I was as appreciative of a Happy Chanukah as a Merry Christmas. We couldn't imagine being offended by either; we were grateful for the thought.

I formed the same friendships attending Bar Mitzvahs or Seders as I did at Confirmation or Easter dinner. They were times to share meaning with friends. These spiritual and social events gave me a better appreciation of Judaism and strengthened my own faith. They fostered friendships that still enrich my life.

I've always found Ben Stein to be an interesting convention speaker and author. Something he recently opined strongly resonates with where I am today. I know the world is a better place when we self-lessly hold convictions like those of Ben Stein. In part, here is what Ben Stein wrote:

> I am a Jew, and every single one of my ancestors was Jewish. And it does not bother me even a little bit when people call those beautiful lit-up, bejeweled trees Christmas trees. I don't feel threatened. I don't feel discriminated against. It doesn't bother me a bit when people say, "Merry Christmas" to me. In fact, I kind of like it. It shows we are all brothers and sisters celebrating this happy time of year. It doesn't bother me at all that there is a manger scene on display at a key intersection near my beach house in Malibu. If people want a crèche, it's just as fine with me as is the Menorah a few hundred yards away.

Chapter Twelve

WINTER ON HUNTING ISLAND

Still round the corner there may wait,
A new road, or a secret gate.

- J.R.R. Tolkien

By most standards, winter is not the best time to visit the Carolina coast. We were still twenty days from spring, but we like the ocean in all seasons and were missing the sea. Eager to spend time on the beach, I picked Andrew up from pre-school on a Wednesday at the beginning of March and we drove to historic Beaufort, South Carolina.

This would be a boy's trip, as Mandy had commitments at school. Arriving in beautiful Beaufort about nine that evening and inquiring at a dozen motels with no success, we grew concerned about lodging. Like our night in Waycross, it was starting to look as if we might have to sleep in the car.

Again we questioned our adventurous approach to lodging. Andrew and I often shun reservations in favor of spontaneity. The reward of arriving without a reservation usually outweighs the shortcomings

– we almost always find interesting places to stay. But on occasion we encounter uncertain moments when everything is booked. These moments serve to reinforce the essential need for planning. They also spark imaginative solutions and nurture our adventurous souls. Encountering sold-out lodgings on a cold night cultivates creativity.

I usually tell Andrew that valuing spontaneity provides an opportunity for forces beyond us to favorably intervene. But this time we discovered it was graduation weekend for the United States Marines at nearby Parris Island. The ceremony for America's finest had brought many families and friends to the area. According to one desk clerk, we'd have more luck finding gold than an available room.

Believing Is Seeing

I moderate a book club that meets each week for a couple of hours. The group is composed of a dozen friends and neighbors who enjoy discussing how the books we read relate to our lives. One evening an associate told me he doubted that God concerns himself with something as ordinary as lodging. The group was evenly split on the issue.

Andrew and I had talked about God's involvement in our lives. That night in Beaufort, as our prospects for a warm bed waned, it seemed like a good time to re-open the issue.

"One person may think God doesn't concern himself with the ordinary events of life, while another may think He is interested in all aspects of our existence," I said. "The first person believes that God is too big to be concerned about people who don't make reservations. We shouldn't be testing God, who has more important things to do.

"The second person believes that God is big enough to do everything, no matter how big or small, and still have time to rest."

It was almost eleven and we were both tired. Passing a bright red

Ramada Inn sign, I concluded my lesson for the evening.

"For the first person, seeing is believing. For the second person, believing is seeing."

Andrew knows from experience that his dad falls into the latter category. He thought it would be fun to sleep in the car, but suggested instead that maybe the Ramada Inn night clerk would let us sleep in the lobby. When we entered the lobby, an attractive young lady was on the phone.

"Do you want a room for tonight?" she asked.

When I nodded eagerly, she turned back to the phone. "There will be no charge; a man here wants your room."

The person on the other end of the line was able to cancel without penalty, and just like that Andrew and I had found our room for the night. Smiling, we agreed to a rate twenty dollars over our budget. Sleeping in the car would have to wait for another time.

As he was getting ready for bed, Andrew asked, "Daddy, do you think Fred Flintstone is healthy?"

I pondered his question. "No, actually I think Fred is overweight. He eats poorly and yells too much."

Andrew weighed my response. "Well, why do you give me his vitamins?"

It was the first time I'd thought about what a poor celebrity endorsement Fred Flintstone is for good health. As I was contemplating an answer, Andrew asked, "Do you think God gave us this room?"

"We did continue to check for rooms, and you suggested the Ramada Inn," I replied. "Continuing to knock on doors indicates that we were keeping the faith against all odds, so yes – I do think He arranged for us to have this room."

"Me too, Dad."

An Ordinary Hero

Our bedtime story that night was about courage and heroism. I told Andrew that heroes often appear to be ordinary people who show the courage to do extraordinary things, or to do ordinary things especially well.

As an example, I told a story about one pleasant Saturday afternoon when I was ten years old. My dad and I were working around the house cutting grass and trimming our hedge. He suggested we call it a day.

"I want to go up to Broward and look at a new housing community," he said. "I'd like your opinion about the subdivision."

Flattered that he wanted my opinion, I readily agreed. We drove east and north on 42 Avenue in our new 1955 Pontiac. Dad had a penchant for a new car every other year, but he was thrifty in his extravagance – he always bought the current model just before the next model year reached the showroom.. I remember telling Dad that I couldn't imagine our attractive turquoise-over-cream wheels ever going out of style. Now, whenever I see a 1955 turquoise-over-cream Pontiac at a car show, my initial feeling is confirmed.

"Andrew," I told my attentive son, "hop in and use your imagination. You can ride with us, but you must be quiet because you're not yet born."

Exchanging smiles, I watched him cross his hands over his lap.

"I'm putting my seat belt on," he said when I asked what he was doing. He was amused to discover that seat belts were not yet standard equipment in 1955-era Pontiacs, not even turquoise-over-cream models.

My dad and I were driving along one of the many deep, wide canals dotting South Florida, about to enter Broward County, when suddenly he looked over at me.

"Did you see that?" he exclaimed.

Neither of us wanted to believe what we had seen. An Oldsmobile had left the road, jumped a dirt mound, and was now quickly submerging into a watery grave. Coming to an abrupt stop, we scampered down the bank toward the murky waters.

The nose of the car was already sinking. An elderly man and a younger woman were in the front seat. Dad ran to the driver's side, yelling, "Nicky, do not go in the canal but help the man get out the window now!"

With water pouring in the front windows, Dad waded into the canal and began struggling to free the young woman who had been driving. She accepted his strong arms, and with great effort he pulled her free. Coughing, she reached the bank.

Tilting dangerously, the large car began slipping away from shore. The older man remained staring out the windshield, stunned, oblivious to my calls. Dad raced around to the passenger side. With the rescued woman screaming for her father to free himself, Dad shouted, "Nicky, grab my hand. We must get him out of the car!"

It was rare to see my normally quiet father so animated. He grabbed the elderly man's arm and yanked. The water in the Olds helped – with my dad pulling on his arms the man floated out the window just as a multitude of gushing air bubbles followed the car's nosedive into a watery grave.

"Andrew, your granddad went into the water and saved two strangers from drowning with no concern for his own well-being. And do you know something else? He didn't know how to swim!"

"Daddy, do you think I will have the courage to be a hero like Granddad?" asked Andrew.

"Yes, I believe you will," I said. Even in the ordinary, believing is seeing. "You are already courageous, and you care for others. Those are the virtues of heroism."

Living Large

The great art of life is sensation, to feel that we exist.

- Lord Byron

Next morning we awoke to a beautiful sunrise. We also discovered that the $20 budget-breaking extravagance of our motel room included a hot breakfast. The cordial lady preparing our eggs asked Andrew what we had planned for the day.

"We didn't have to sleep in the car last night," Andrew grinned happily, "and today we're going to the beach."

Making our way to Hunting Island State Park via the Beaufort Marina, we decided to spring for a ride in a horse-drawn carriage. Our scholarly guide described the important role the historic city of Beaufort had played in the revolutionary and civil wars. The history wasn't nearly as interesting to my five-year-old as the friendly Spaniel on the driver's bench. When Andrew reached over to pet the dog, the Spaniel reacted with friendly licks.

The large, sturdy steed methodically pulling the carriage had obviously followed the route many times and needed little guidance negotiating the narrow byways of Beaufort. Our tour took us underneath grand old Spanish-moss-adorned oaks and past stately homes – the movie *The Big Chill* was filmed in one of the larger homes on the route – and afforded wonderful views of the ocean. Again petting the Spaniel and horse, we departed the carriage convinced of the therapeutic value of being around such affable and gentle creatures, and wiser about the history of Beaufort.

Crossing the bridge on Highway 21 that weds Beaufort to Lady's Island, flowing with the beauty of the Broad, Beaufort and Coosa Rivers, passing more old oaks trees and an interesting variety of properties with wonderful views of the waterways and sea-going vessels, we eventually arrived at Hunting Island State Park and the always-awesome Atlantic Ocean. It boded well for a pleasant day on Hunting Island Beach.

The Atlantic was invigoratingly chilly as Andrew and I removed our shoes. Walking along the unspoiled beach, we came across fallen trees eroded by the eternal waves. A helpful park ranger told us that what Mother Nature was removing from the Atlantic side she was replacing on the leeward side. Andrew found this interesting – islands, like all of life, are ever-changing. I made a mental note to research tides on the internet – the ranger's comments were already cultivating questions for which I had no answers.

Shrieking with excitement as the frigid water splashed his legs and soaked his shorts, Andrew ran from the surf to the prostrate, sun-bleached trees, then back to the beach. Among his many discoveries were a Horseshoe Crab and a six-foot plank, obviously from a pirate ship. The latter led to a guarded search of the horizon, half-hoping to see the rest of the ship and its crew, and half-terrified that we would.

Encountering only a few others that inspiring morning except for the natural inhabitants of a pristine beach and an unblemished pine forest, we felt far away from the usual hustle of life. Closer to the eternal, we felt energized at a deep, lasting level.

A few hours later we returned to the parking area, where our attention was captured by the impressive 1874 Hunting Island lighthouse. Upon closer inspection, we determined that it was open. Climbing all 170 steps, Andrew with considerably less effort than me, we arrived at the top. Standing on exhausted, wobbly legs I could see where we had driven that morning and beyond that a panoramic vista of the 5,000-acre island. From our precarious perch atop the aged structure we looked out over miles of ocean and shore bathed in warm, noon-hour sunlight delivered on cool breezes. A spectacular sight, it further lifted our spirits. Whooping triumphantly, Andrew raised a clenched fist.

"This is awesome, Daddy!"

There was more to see in the park. At every turn we were encouraged to explore. Hiking trails winding through a primitive maritime forest took us to a saltwater marsh and a fishing pier. We were delighted when a raccoon and her offspring crossed our path. With only a cursory look at us they hurried by, apparently convinced of better things ahead.

The wonderfully blustery weather was too tumultuous for fishing, but it made for great excitement venturing from the pier house to the end of the pier. Laughing and shouting jubilantly as the winds roughed us up, we returned to the pier house and found a discovery center with many interesting sea creatures.

Island Hopping

Returning to the motel, we decided to dine on rustic Port Royal Island. We chose a restaurant with tables overlooking the shrimp boats on Port Royal Sound. Andrew asked if we could run along the docks after dinner. Our meal of fresh flounder was tasty, but anticipating our run we didn't linger. With the sun setting, we ventured along the waterfront past weathered docks and romantic shrimp boats, convinced that many interesting stories remained to be told about mariners stoically scratching out a living on their old vessels.

In times past, I told Andrew, pirates had also visited Port Royal Island. As darkness prevailed, we wondered if their descendants would appear. We wouldn't be the first innocents to be carried off to sea and forced into a life of piracy. As it got darker we walked softer, contemplating the point at which bravery and folly diverge.

Safely back in our car, it was time to return to our favorite place – home. Driving north on Highway 21 from Beaufort, anticipating that somewhere up the road would be an interesting place to spend the night, Andrew wanted to tell Mandy about our fun day. Hitting the speed dial on the cell phone, he left a voice-mail message.

"Mommy, we had a really great time. The last bathroom had an overflowed toilet and there was water everywhere. I love you. Bye."

Passion in All Seasons

Andrew is a naturally high-energy, optimistic, confident child. From an early age he has shown an enthusiasm for life that is gratifying, sometimes tiring, and often entertaining. Mandy and I encourage our son's passion. To this end we recently read a fascinating book, *No More Christian Nice Guy: When Being Nice Instead of Good Hurts Men, Women, and Children*. Author Paul Coughlin includes quotes from two writers whose works and values have most favorably endured the test of time:

"The happiness of a man in this life does not consist in the absence but in the mastery of his passions," Alfred Lord Tennyson noted.

"It would seem that our Lord finds our desires not too strong, but too weak. We are half-hearted creatures, fooling about with drink and sex and ambition when infinite joy is offered us, like an ignorant child who wants to go on making mud pies in a slum because he cannot imagine what is meant by the offer of a holiday at the sea. We are far too easily pleased." C. S. Lewis wrote that passage in *The Weight of Glory.*

We want Andrew to understand that he, like all children, is uniquely blessed with certain talents. His talents are foundational to what he can do with his life. Regardless of circumstance, every child is born uniquely special, with specific talents intended for a purposeful life.

To visualize what inspires him, we've helped Andrew start a scrapbook. Already the photo album includes images of family and friends, astronauts, trains, mountains, oceans and a library. There are also pictures of a homeless person, a dilapidated car and a storm-ravaged house – there is no escaping the fact that life brings sorrow as well as happiness. A successful life is determined not in escaping vicissitudes, but in feeling and dealing with them. While meaningful lives are found in corporate boardrooms, they are also found in bathing the indigent. May the love and guidance we give our children provide them with the courage to express passion in all of their seasons. May we feel God's favor in rediscovering our own worthy passions.

> To everything there is a season.
> A time for every purpose under heaven:
> A time to be born,
> And a time to die;
> A time to plant,
> And a time to pluck what is planted;
> A time to kill,
> And a time to heal;
> A time to break down,
> And a time to build up;
> A time to weep,
> And a time to laugh;
> A time to mourn,
> And a time to dance;

A time to cast away stones;
And a to embrace,
And a time to refrain from embracing;
A time to gain,
And a time to lose;
A time to keep;
And a time to throw away;
A time to tear,
And a time to sew;
A time to keep silence,
And a time to speak;
A time to love,
And a time for hate;
A time of war,
And a time of peace.

- Ecclesiastes 3: 1-8

Chapter Thirteen

PONCHOS AND SALSA

I am a part of all that I have met.

- Alfred Lord Tennyson

Harmony in History

The town of Lumpkin is located not too far south of Columbus, Georgia, not too far east of Eufaula, Alabama, and a world away from Atlanta. Leaving Highway 27 and entering the town square, we felt like we had driven decades back into a kinder, gentler time.

Mandy, Andrew and I were spending our spring break at Providence Canyon State Park near Lumpkin, and after driving all morning we decided to stop for lunch. Selecting Leslie's Café, one of the two restaurants in town, we each chose a fried chicken breast and three of the many savory vegetables.

Meat and threes are some of our favorite places to eat. For special occasions we prefer Ruth's Chris Steak Houses, which have an excellent choice of fresh vegetables, but Ruth's doesn't have delicious field pies, collards or cornbread on their menu. Sitting at a table by the window, we politely watched the folks of Lumpkin going about their business.

The men we saw wore everything from bib overalls to business suits. The women were pleasantly groomed and dressed but we noticed there were no designer threads, nor were there hair curlers, Nike runners or flip-flops. If clothes do indeed make the person, it appeared that these people were comfortable with themselves, and with their community.

An older gentleman entered the restaurant. He was obviously liked and respected. Removing his straw hat and placing it on the rack by the door, he was warmly greeted with smiles and humor. We were struck by the establishment's feeling of country contentment. It was contagious.

After an enjoyable lunch, we reluctantly left the Lumpkin town square heading toward Westville. We only drove a couple of miles, but we found ourselves back a hundred years in time.

Two Mules, an Old Man and a Boy

Westville is a self-described functioning living history village. The town's relocated, restored and recaptured buildings realistically portray small-town culture in the mid-1800s.

Andrew was impressed with almost all aspects of the village. He was particularly taken with his ride down a dirt road in a buckboard pulled by two mules. Sitting in the front seat beside an old man holding the reins, Andrew was thrilled by the power of the sturdy mules and by the sounds of the creaking wagon and the clanging blacksmith's hammer.

The village sounds prevented me from hearing the quiet conversation between Andrew and the elderly gentleman, but it was evident that he was imparting the wisdom of the ages. The child was eager to learn, occasionally looking up at the old man with the respect and interest children generally reserve for their grandparents. The old man's hands were steady as the mules instinctively traveled the twenty-minute journey around the village. As the old man captured our son's imagination Mandy and I looked on, observing the poignant interaction with heartwarming pleasure. Andrew readily accepted our offer of a second trip around the village. We sat in the back, savoring the experience.

Later we didn't feel it appropriate to pry. Andrew didn't offer much more, other than to say he liked the man. I did tell Andrew that the word of the day was poignant. I said perhaps one day we'd write a short story and call it *Two Mules, an Old Man and a Boy*. It would be a poignant story about lessons of life learned on a buckboard.

Yes, We Have No Nachos

Leaving Westville with a better appreciation of historic Georgia and the people who laid the foundations for those who followed, we drove thirty miles to Columbus and our room for the night. We'd drive back to visit Providence Canyon State Park the following day.

On the way to Columbus it started to rain, so Mandy suggested we stop and get some ponchos. We didn't want to postpone our canyon hike if the rain continued. Stopping at a dollar store, Mandy returned with three gaudy orange raincoats. Andrew and I looked at them in disbelief.

"Why didn't you get the ugly ones?" I asked.

Andrew was puzzled too, but for a different reason. "Where's the nachos?" he wondered.

By the time we had dinner and settled down for a good night's sleep, it was late. I started to doze off, chuckling about poncho-nacho confusion, when Andrew sat up.

"Dad, we didn't do a lesson today."

"I read you a bedtime story."

"I know, but we didn't do a lesson."

It was almost ten-thirty. Mandy was already asleep. Wearily, I put my shoes on and hoofed it out to the car to retrieve our latest School Specialty Children's Publishing book. These interesting books cover a wide variety of learning materials for students in pre-school through Grade Six. We purchase them at Sam's for less than half their retail cost. Fun learning tools, they provide an opportunity to talk and to spend time together.

One of the joys of raising Andrew is his eagerness to learn – even when his passion is kindled after bedtime.

Immortal Pleasures

Our Creator would never have made such lovely days and given us the deep hearts to enjoy them unless we were meant to be immortal.

- Nathaniel Hawthorne

The next morning while driving to Providence Canyon State Park Andrew wanted to play the game where I ask him questions. After fielding many easy questions, he wanted a hard one.

"What are the four seasons?" I asked.

Andrew thought hard. As a hint, Mandy suggested he think of Thanksgiving, Christmas, planting our garden and cookouts. Pondering a little longer, Andrew finally responded.

"I can only think of two – salt and pepper."

With the sun rising on the promise of another wondrous day, we entered Providence Canyon State Park. Two marked trails meander through the thousand-acre park – one trail is three miles long, and the other trail is seven miles. Agreeing to save the longer and more difficult path for another day, we chose the three-mile hike.

It was immediately evident that this would be another great day in nature. The soil in the park's canyon comes in a variety of interesting colors, ranging from sandy white to red and purple. In springtime, the colorful soil is complemented by flowering trees, Azaleas and wildflowers – all offering a wonderful visual feast.

Providence Canyon is known as the Little Grand Canyon. The three-mile trail hugs the rim and provides spectacularly expansive panoramic views across the top and all the way down to the distant canyon floor. The trail is marked as rugged because much of the three miles is covered with the roots of mature trees, but I would rate it as moderate even for a five-year-old. We took many deep breaths of the marvelously fragrant fresh air, filling our lungs with the healing balm. Andrew had the time of his life hiking through the interesting surroundings and negotiating a couple of creeks, while Mandy and I reveled in our son's excitement.

One of the many rewards of fostering a happy child is that the happiness is contagious. The creek-crossings clearly necessitated removing our shoes to feel the cool water. The combination of moist red clay and sand squishing between our toes prompted shrieks of joy from our pre-schooler. Like most boys, Andrew feels he must place his feet in every body of water he encounters, from puddles and creeks to oceans, to confirm that they are indeed the wet kind. In case you haven't noticed, no child can possibly roll up his pant legs high enough to keep them dry – this is one of the unofficial laws of nature.

After enjoying the first creek we replaced our shoes and came across some rusted-out abandoned cars. Choosing to believe that the derelict autos belonged to moonshiners, we shivered at the thought of encountering outlaws on the trail. Equating them to pirates, Andrew wanted to know the probability of seeing an actual moonshiner, and looked nervous when I affirmed that there might still be some in the area. Stepping lighter after that, we began to hear and see many intriguing things in the forest. Some of them may even have been outlaws. Soon, however, other fascinating things caught our attention and the possibility of a chance encounter with desperados slipped away.

We weren't tired, but our senses were being wonderfully treated by our surroundings and we wanted to linger, savoring the moment. Stopping along the trail, we breathed in the heavenly fragrances. Watching hawks gliding gracefully on the wind currents and listening to songbirds singing gleefully in the trees, we felt that nature was enriching our lives. Embracing our immortality we continued walking, and eventually came full circle back to our starting point.

Thanking the park ranger who showed us a bumble bee colony adjacent to the interpretive center, we assured her that we'd return next spring to backpack the seven-mile trail and perhaps even to use the pioneer campground. I knew we would do the hike, but I was less sure about the camping. I'd like to say it's about Mandy. But the truth is that our whole family, including Dawn and Kimberly, thinks roughing it is a room that doesn't include a complementary breakfast.

A Fish Story

April has put a spirit of youth in everything.

- William Shakespeare

Leaving Providence Canyon and heading west to Florence State Park and Marina, still appreciating all the wonders of that awesome April day, Andrew asked for a story about my childhood.

"This is about the time I caught a rather large fish in Key West," I began. "We were on a boy's outing with Little River Baptist Church. It was my only catch in a full day of fishing, but it was the largest fish I ever caught."

One of the councilors complimented me on my catch. After photographing the great fish, he told me to toss it back in the ocean. We'd soon be packing for the four-hour bus ride back to Miami. I badly wanted my family to see what I landed, and thought it fortuitous when the councilor was distracted away. Quickly wrapping the fish in a large towel and then a blanket, I stealthily placed the bundle in my duffle bag.

It was a long, hot, humid South Florida day. We returned from Key West to North Miami on a bus with no air conditioning. I arrived home too late to unpack. Leaving my prize in the duffle bag, it remained there until the next day – after Sunday school, after church and after dinner.

Mandy enjoys hearing these stories about my life. It's her way of confirming that I married up. She and Andrew renewed their laughter as I refreshed their memories about the ire of my parents when they finally discovered my catch and later – much later – their laughter. To this day I never smell spoiling fish without remembering the story of my biggest catch.

Florence State Park has half a dozen cottages, eight efficiencies, boat slips, a fishing pier, a swimming pool and lots of natural space. Impressed, we vowed to stay there on our next visit. The park is located on 45,000-acre Lake Eufaula in Alabama, one of the best prize bass lakes anywhere. You may catch and release or, if you wish, you can wrap your catch in a towel and store it in a duffle bag.

For us, it was too late to go fishing. Under a marvelous setting sun we removed our shoes and found a place to dangle our feet in the soothing water, mesmerized by the colorful sunset and grateful for another shared day of simple pleasures.

Obnoxious, Self-Absorbed and Unrefined

*Humor helps us to realize that from God's point of view
the self-important human being is a pretty funny creature!*
- C.S. Lewis

Darkness had fallen when we began to drive home. Stopping for dinner in Columbus, we found an Italian restaurant and ordered pizza. We were soon joined by other patrons in observing a woman at the next table noisily devouring her meal without missing a beat in her completely self-absorbed conversation. Actually, conversation is the wrong word. Inane speech would be a better description. She appeared to be with three generations of her family – her mother, husband and children – all of whom were dazed by her monologue.

Too important to turn off her cell phone, between bites she responded several times to calls. Watching her eating and talking did more to convince Andrew to chew with his mouth closed than anything I'd ever said. It also underscored the virtue of listening. Loud and preoccupied, she didn't realize she was the center of attention far beyond her table. Her imposing crassness had everyone looking on in disbelief.

The moment we entered the sanctuary of our car Mandy, Andrew and I erupted in laughter. We laughed not at the woman or her beleaguered family, but in the folly of her prideful self-indulgence.

Somewhere near Newnan in a sparsely populated area we decided to stop for a moment. Stretching our legs, feeling the dampness of the night air and observing the expansive starlit sky, we gazed with wonder and amazement at the heavens. Mandy and I pointed out the North Star as well as the Big Dipper and the Little Dipper. This was the extent of our astrological prowess. Andrew, as usual, came up with a stumper.

"Where's the medium dipper?"

Chapter Fourteen

COURTING PERIL

I came to the conclusion that the Optimist thought everything good except the Pessimist, and that the Pessimist thought everything bad except himself.

- G.K. Chesterton

One day picking Andrew up from pre-school I found him quieter than his usual animated self. When I asked what he had learned that day, he was silent. After a minute or so, I repeated the question.

"What did you learn in school today?"

"Dad, I didn't learn anything," my pensive son replied.

"You spent the whole day in school and didn't learn anything?"

"Yes. I guess that's why I have to keep going back."

At home Andrew asked for my Plate of Pasta story. Sitting in our comfortable living room recliner, basking in the warmth of the afternoon sun, I clarified that he meant my analogy about the

Italian dinner and the meaning of life.

"A successful life is not unlike a savory Italian dinner. Which ingredient do we value above the rest? Is it the fresh tomatoes or the celery; the basil or the lean ground beef? Is it the olive oil, the Chianti or the bread? Is it the operatic music playing in the background? Or is it the sumptuous marriage of all these ingredients combined that we savor?"

Understanding from previous renditions that my questions were rhetorical, Andrew remained contemplative and quietly attentive. I continued.

"The preparation is like working in a generous garden. It is a labor of love, including chopping the onion and the garlic. Is it the mincing of these two miracle bulbs that brings tears to our eyes, or is it Russell Watson's moving song *Amore Musica*?"

I was just getting wound up, waxing enthusiastic and ready to launch into my overture, which is about the cooking and the fine art of living well, when Andrew interrupted.

"I think it's everything, but I don't want to chop the garlic and onions!"

I haven't researched my Italian and Scottish heritage, but Andrew and I frequently belt out *I Te Vurria Vasa* in Italian and *You'll Still Be There for Me* from the movie *Rob Roy*. We sing with all the passion of an Italian and the enthusiasm of a Scotsman – albeit a few beats behind the accomplished virtuosos who perform those tunes professionally.

My Italian heritage does not include the ability to speak the language. I know only a few words that Grandpa Lore taught me when I was Andrew's age. Grandpa Lore had a wonderful work ethic and he helped me appreciate the joys of working in a home garden. These days it is me teaching Andrew to enjoy laboring in our lakeside garden with all of its fragrances and rewards such as apples and blueberries that we harvest and share with the birds and bees.

I believe it is important that Andrew appreciate his heritage. Every child should understand the meaning of his roots. But I do not encourage Andrew to embrace hyphenated cultures like Italian-American or Scottish-American. There are so many opportunities in America. I encourage Andrew to value his heritage while at the same time understanding that he is blessed to be an American. The only hyphenating I encourage is in the term All-American. I pray that Andrew will know the humility and happiness of God's pleasure in his life, and that one day if he so desires he will achieve that pinnacle of accomplishment.

Our discussion about healthy Italian dinners led to preparing one on Saturday afternoon, in advance of our Mother's Day dinner the next evening. Preparing the tasty, nutritious ingredients, we placed them in our crock pot. The next morning we awoke to a wonderful bouquet of Italian aromas. Yielding to temptation, Mandy, Andrew and I heartily consumed a savory bowl of pasta primavera for breakfast, then proceeded to church laughing and reeking of garlic. We doubted we'd have to share our pew with a werewolf that day.

Humility and Pride

Pride is a weakness in the character, it dries up laughter, it dries up wonder, it dries up chivalry and energy
- G.K. Chesterton

Inspired by the sermon that morning, after church we talked about humility. We show respect and humility when we care enough to have genuine interest in others. Humility is the ability to listen to others with empathy. We talked about how too many people spend inordinate amounts of time attempting to evaluate how virtually everything will affect them. We call these people Boring Bob and Paul Pride, and we contrast them with our hero, Harry Havefun.

Paul Pride is enslaved by his own self-importance. He takes credit for what goes well and blames others for what does not. He is unaccountable and miserable. Even when Paul shows a glimmer of humility he quickly becomes proud of it. He takes pride in the virtue of humility.

Boring Bob has no interest beyond himself. Bob is easily offended, holds a grudge and lacks a sense of humor. In particular, he lacks the ability to laugh at himself. The pride of his self-importance, which he loathes to admit, shackles him to a joyless existence. He's the monkey with his hand in the cookie jar unwilling to let go of all that makes him unhappy.

Conversely, Harry Havefun reaches out to others with a listening ear and a helping hand. Harry knows the joy that comes from understanding how much more can be accomplished, and how much more can be appreciated, by being selfless. Harry is honest. He sets goals beyond what is in it for him.

I realize this is pretty heavy stuff for a five-year-old, but Andrew relishes stories with life-lessons. It is most gratifying and rewarding to know that Andrew is interested in ideas and people beyond himself. When I was a student at Miami Norland High School my favorite teacher, Mrs. Jasaki, impressed the following upon me: "Boring people talk about themselves, average people talk about others, and leaders discuss ideas so they can take appropriate action."

Mandy, Andrew and I admire and revere Mother Theresa, who was an ambassador of goodwill and selflessness as well as a Nobel Laureate, not for any single significant event such as discovering a cure or achieving a monumental milestone, but for her multitude of simple acts. For most of the eighty-seven years of her heroic life she epitomized humble service. She was propelled to aid scores of hapless people by her love of God. She knew the downtrodden could never repay her efforts on this side of heaven.

Andrew understands that Harry Havefun, like Mother Theresa, is liberated because he has humility and a genuine interest in others. I'm always heartened at how easy it is for Andrew to interact with other children. His engaging manner confirms that a person who is comfortable in his own neighborhood will readily make friends across town and beyond. When we travel, many of our rest stops include children's playgrounds. It's particularly interesting to observe children who do not share a common language play together. Young children apparently have developed a universal language for games like hide-and-seek, or tag. Life is better when we embrace a variety of people, places and things.

A Bit Careless

The paradox of courage is that a man must be a little careless of his life even in order to keep it.
- *G.K. Chesterton*

One day hiking back from visiting a waterfall Andrew asked if he could run ahead. I agreed as long as he didn't scamper out of my sight. Accepting my condition, he nimbly ran ahead. I knew this would concern Mandy and many other mothers, but I also knew that most boys crave possible peril.

On the constantly curving trail, my stay-in-sight rule meant that Andrew would never be more than fifty feet from me. It is a father's responsibility to help his son understand and manage risk. Courage comes when a child learns to face fear, and it arrives early in life. In courage a boy begins to embrace his manhood. Courage is foundational to all other virtues. I understood my son's need for the excitement of danger.

Running ahead, Andrew came to an abrupt stop. He looked hard at something on the path. Wheeling around, he shouted with more interest than alarm, "Daddy, there's a snake!"

Exhorting him to keep his distance, I ran to Andrew's side. A two-foot Copperhead Snake basking in a ray of sunlight tricking through the canopy of trees was not the least bit threatened by us. Curled up in the middle of the narrow trail, it was obviously enjoying the warmth. It wasn't advisable to pass on either side of the serpent. We waited a few minutes but the creature refused to budge, so we retraced our steps seeking a lengthy stick. I picked up a long branch (long is the operative word) and began pruning the twigs.

"Daddy, please don't hurt it!" Andrew pleaded.

Assuring my naturalist son that my only intent was to move the reptile as long as it remained amenable, I cautiously slid the branch under the snake and raised it just high enough to move it from the path. We adroitly and respectfully passed with Andrew safely perched on my shoulders. Our chance meeting with one of nature's more intriguing creatures provided a special moment for us, and a small lesson in courage.

Rhythm of the Rain

Our Copperhead Snake encounter had distracted us from the dark clouds and rolling thunder, but now an awesome flash of lightening startled us with its nearness. All at once the densely clouded skies opened up and a torrential downpour became cause for concern. Picking up our pace as the rain intensified, another bolt of lightening crackled uncomfortably near. We came to a tiny, antiquated cabin. Anticipating a warm reception and refuge from the ominous storm, we approached the diminutive structure.

Our knock at the cabin door generated no response, but we chanced sitting on the gently twisted, worn timber of the chair-less porch. Hoping we were not trespassing, we positioned ourselves almost out of reach of the rain. Resting our backs against the wall, Andrew leaned against me.

"Daddy, this is wonderful!" Andrew shouted to make himself heard over the storm.

I nodded. "How fortunate are we?"

"Very!"

It was indeed wonderful – the rain had cooled the late afternoon, and the earth offered up marvelously soothing aromas conducive to meditative thought and reflection. Spectacular bolts of lightening flashed across the heavens, with thunder closely following. The trees swayed and the leaves danced to the rhythm of the rain on the ancient tin roof. Sitting contemplatively, we were quietly grateful for our refuge and equally thankful for the storm that had provided us with this time for thought. We spoke little during our hour on the porch, but we communed mightily.

A Good Plan

After a while the storm subsided. Leaving our humble shelter in waning daylight, Andrew let me know in no uncertain terms that he was ready to eat. I recalled going to an Atlanta Thrashers hockey game the previous week. Andrew's comment reminded me of his dinner at the hockey game.

Ron Tuckley, my former father-in-law, had come to visit from his home in Toddington, England. A spry eighty-five-year-old English gentleman who Andrew affectionately calls Tuckley, his visit was another special opportunity for Andrew, who came to appreciate a person, a time and a place he might otherwise never have known.

Our limited knowledge about the game of hockey was offset by the excitement of the Atlanta Thrashers six-three win over the Florida Panthers. Tuckley is not a fan of American fast food. With no Shepherd's Pie or fish and chips on the menu at Philips Arena, we decided to feast on bread pretzels, popcorn and a beverage. Soon after we started our questionable culinary delight I looked over at my son. His pail of popcorn and large bread pretzel completely concealed his lap, and his root beer float toggled back and forth from cup-holder to mouth.

Catching my glance, Andrew intuitively understood that I had reservations about his fatty, sugary, salty, three-course meal. Giving me a great big smile, he said, "Daddy, this is the best dinner I've ever had!"

Thinking how good a three-course hockey game meal would taste right now, we continued hiking. A mile from the trailhead and our car, we came to a creek. We had easily negotiated it on our hike in but now, after the rainstorm, negotiating safe passage required some thought. What a few hours before had taken only a good jump now necessitated crossing a deep, wide, turbulent stream.

Discussing our options, we settled on hopping across three large river rocks scarcely elevated above the white water. Our plan was for me to go first. I would secure a footing on each rock, then turn and help Andrew. Two rocks into our three-rock obstacle course we reached the middle. So far, so good. Suddenly, without any hope of recovery, I started sliding off the boulder, unintentionally pulling my son down with me. Gasping for breath at the icy shock, we found ourselves struggling against the tumultuous current, fighting to free ourselves from the swollen water. Cold and spent when we reached the bank; we sat for a moment laughingly imagining how inept we must have looked while poorly implementing our well-thought-out plan.

"Next time I'll go first," said Andrew.

I'm a fortunate father to have the uncomplaining companion-ship of an adventurous son like Andrew. Continuing our assault on the trailhead, soaking wet, numbed by the frigid water and less confident in our hiking prowess, we still managed to retain a sense of humor.

Darkness had prevailed when we finally reached the car. Turning on the heater, we drove the narrow gravel road in silence. Some days are unremarkable, while others are deeply felt. A successful life is one in which more days are deeply felt. As we turned onto the paved road and headed for home, I handed Andrew the cell phone and asked him to call Mandy so she wouldn't worry about our lateness. He hit the speed dial.

"Mommy, we moved a snake and fell in a creek. It was a great!"

Holy Land

A fool and his money are easily parted.

- *Thomas Tusser*

Our going-home story, by popular request, was about an episode I had shared with Kimberly when she graduated from high school. My oldest daughter, Dawn, had chosen a fine watch for her gradu-ation gift, but Kimberly chose a trip to the Holy Land.

As Kimberly and I exited the Tel Aviv International Airport, we saw that everything was closed. We needed change for a taxi ride into Jerusalem, and began looking for a place to convert one of our $100 American bills into small-denomination Israeli currency.

A kind soul approached and asked if he could help. I explained our situation. He confirmed that neither the exchange kiosk in the airport nor the banks would open for some time. The well-dressed man was clearly concerned for us, and as we talked I gained confidence in him.

He had the opposite effect on my daughter. Disappointed in Kimberly's body language and her cynical expression, I decided to give my skeptical daughter a valuable lesson in trust. I wanted her to be more trusting of her fellow human beings.

Agreeing to wait at the airport entrance, I handed the good Samaritan my $100 bill. He said he would return in ten minutes with the appropriate change. I offered but he graciously declined a fee for his service, explaining that his brother would open his bank early for him. It made sense to me. Kimberly rolled her eyes as he departed for his brother's bank, walking at first and then quickening his pace before running out of sight.

We waited twenty minutes. My annoyance with my suspicious daughter was soon replaced by uneasiness. I pondered the man's hasty disappearance. I loathed the thought of admitting that the lesson would not be for my daughter, but for me. Could it be true that even in the land of Abraham, Isaac, Jacob and Jesus the foolish get fleeced? Finally I looked at Kimberly.

"I don't think he's coming back."

"Oh, really?" she replied dryly.

Chapter Fifteen

CALLAWAY GARDENS

The really wonderful moments of joy in this world are not the moments of self-satisfaction, but self-forgetfulness. Standing on the edge of the Grand Canyon and contemplating your own greatness is pathological. At such moments we are made for a magnificent joy that comes from outside ourselves.

- John Piper

Callaway Gardens is a naturally beautiful place. When Andrew first visited the gardens on his second Christmas with his sisters Kimberly and Dawn, and Dawn's family, the holiday music and Fantasy In Lights Christmas show featuring more than eight million lights (I didn't personally count them all) raised our spirits and warmed our souls.

Now we were returning for Andrew's fourth visit. At five, he'd better appreciate the variety of colors that provide a special Callaway treat no matter what time of year. We savor the gardens in all four seasons. My favorite two seasons there are fall, when the cooler temperatures provide relief from the hot Georgia summer; and spring, when the multi-colored azaleas and dogwoods are in full blossom among the natural woodlands.

This time it was late spring, and the dogwoods and azaleas in full bloom provided an awesome celebration of fragrances and colors. The different varieties of flowering plants presented a full spectrum of heavenly hues and fragrances.

Whenever we visit Callaway Gardens we make sure to include ample time to hike, ride bikes, swim at the lakeside beach and stroll through the gardens, including the Cecil B. Day Butterfly Center. We also enjoy the Resort at Callaway where golf, tennis and fishing are available.

On days like this, when we are out exploring, it's always reward-ing to ask Andrew what he sees and what he is thinking. A child's unbridled energy, optimism and inquisitiveness are daily celebra-tions of life. Whenever I make the effort to see things through my son's eyes I, too, see more. My perceptions, like Andrew's, become fresh and exciting.

I pray that all parents will appreciate the specialness of their children, encouraging them to discover, develop and use their God-given gifts. Very few people like Tiger Woods exist in this world – people who can perform at the highest level and be clearly the best. But there are also no ordinary people. Every child, and every person, can do his or her best. Every person can make a meaningful contribution. This is true even – perhaps especially – in the little things.

Andrew understands that we must guard against any feelings that serve to minimize the gifts and specialness of others. There is joy in appreciating the uniqueness of others. It is incumbent on us, as parents, to impress upon our children that they are unique, and to encourage them to see uniqueness in others. This leads to content-ment beyond ourselves, beyond our circumstances.

It often appears to me that the most unfulfilled people are those who have the most things. Tommy Toyboy, another of our improvised characters, has more toys than anyone else yet finds no contentment in what he has. He has only an insatiable desire for more.

Curative Conversational Camaraderie

One Saturday morning soon after Andrew was born, my walking club drove down to Callaway Gardens. There were five of us at the time, and just for fun we decided to change our venue. Recalling the occasion with fondness, I told Andrew the story.

Andrew likes all of the guys in our current walking group and occasionally rides his Razor scooter or bike with us when we walk. He understands the value of walking and talking, of reading and discussing, and of just simply being around good folks. He is most taken by the camaraderie of family and friends; his favorite stories are always about our exploits. He liked my story of our excursion to Callaway, and wanted to hear more about my walking groups.

Early in my adult life I started informal groups for running and more formal groups for talking. The latter often took the form of book clubs. My activities in this area continue to this day, and I am better for them. When we improve our own lives, we improve the lives of those around us.

Spending time with others is attempting to hold on to an important but dying tradition. It hasn't been that long since families and friends regularly gathered on front porches to visit and talk. It was a time to listen, and to be listened to. We were all better for our conversations and for our time together. Today, too many of us don't even talk to our neighbors beyond an occasional greeting while collecting the mail.

My current book club averages about twelve members. We use the works of C.S. Lewis to foster conversation and camaraderie, and we value our time together. A current core group of four members walks about three miles in under an hour every morning in one of the many nearby parks. As we walk, we talk about a variety of topics, most of which we know little about. Our ability to wax eloquently on almost any subject is rarely clouded by what we actually know.

This time together helps us avoid the modern trend of paying professionals for a diagnosis and prescription. Four months after joining our walk-and-talk group one of our members, Skip Johnson, was taken off his diabetes medication. It hasn't been all smooth sailing, though. One of our city council members, George Sipe, showed up for his maiden walk with two little Shih-Tzu pups. When our fourth member arrived late the next day Skip and I voted him the duty of telling George we were walking, not herding puppies.

The Cleaning Lady's Husband

The morning after our arrival at Callaway we decided to share breakfast in a rustic little restaurant in the quaint town of Pine Mountain. Over breakfast we had time for a story. I told Andrew it didn't have much of a moral, but I thought he might find it funny.

After my divorce Dawn, Kimberly and I had done our best to keep our Emerald Hills condominium clean, but within a few weeks it was clear that we needed professional help. Asking around, I secured the number of Marilyn, a lady reputed to keep her client's homes immaculate. We agreed on a weekly Friday-afternoon schedule and on the first day Marilyn proved worthy of a Mr. Clean award. Andrew smiled at that analogy.

"Is that the funny part?" he asked.

I told him to be patient – it got better. Returning to his chocolate-chip pancakes, he listened closely. He is a seasoned story-listener, and the pressure I felt was intense.

At the end of her first afternoon Marilyn observed that there was more work than she could properly do in one afternoon. "Mr. Lore, the wrap-around porch is just more than I anticipated," she said. Her other commitments precluded her from spending more time at our place, but she had a suggestion.

"Sometimes my husband helps me. He can do the mopping and dusting while I concentrate on the rest of the work."

I thought it was a good solution, and we agreed on an additional fee. As Marilyn was heading out the door I thought of something I had forgotten to ask.

"Marilyn, what's your husband's name?"

"His name is Bill, but we call him Dusty."

Andrew scrunched his nose for a moment, considering her response. Then he gave me three out of five on the laugh meter. I knew I'd have to do better next time.

Allergic to Oatmeal

Making our way back to Callaway for a day of hiking and exploring, Andrew thanked me for allowing him to avoid any portion of my breakfast. His nemesis is oatmeal. Early last summer he had chucked up a couple of bowls of porridge soon after eating them, and we had decreed that from then on his culinary repertoire would not include oatmeal.

"It appears that you are allergic to oatmeal," I had said. "You won't have to eat it again."

Attempting to clarify just what kind of blessing would permit him to remove mush from his menu, he asked many questions. I explained that an allergy is something your body reacts poorly to, or rejects. Most people avoid things they are allergic to. Some people have lots of allergies, while others have few or none, I said.

Somewhere in my subliminal consciousness it was vaguely apparent that our discussion was being processed and stored, one day to return. Soon after starting pre-school in September Miss Anita, Andrew's teacher, wrote a note in his school correspondence folder.

"Dear Nick and Mandy:

I regret to inform you that Andrew advised me today he is allergic to writing."

She further explained that Andrew's self-diagnosis included a prognosis that his allergic condition would improve with more time on the playground. Miss Anita's sense of humor often won the day, but there was no frivolity in Andrew's mind. He was most serious about his attempt to avoid writing. Mandy said it sounded like we were raising a doctor, but I assured her that these were merely the early signs of a good salesman.

"Good try, but no cigar," I told my son. This required yet another explanation.

The Virtue of Being Still

Callaway Gardens was great fun. Our senses were wonderfully treated to the multitude of sounds, fragrances and colors. Reading the informative signage, Andrew learned the difference between deciduous trees, evergreens and conifers. After several miles of hiking and climbing, toward the end of the afternoon we found a stately, venerable oak. Easing our tired backs against the sturdy trunk, we lazily accepted the tree's gracious hospitality for a moment of quiet repose. Sitting and resting under its expansive branches, we reflected on a most wonderful day.

"Daddy, how old is this tree?" Andrew asked.

"I'd say it's been offering sanctuary for over a hundred years," I replied.

Pleasantly spent, we savored the setting sun and the cooling breeze gently flowing through the leaves. In front of us was a spectacular kaleidoscope of sparkling sight and sound. I was especially taken with the aural blessings – even the greatest composers can only hope to portray the sounds of nature in the very best of their compositions. In my opinion, the most wondrous of all natural sounds are the pounding of ocean waves, pouring rain and a breeze finding its way through leaves. These priceless auditory experiences require only the virtue of being still.

"I bet Antonio Vivaldi was inspired by days such as this when he wrote The Four Seasons," I said.

"Do you think he ever visited Callaway Gardens?"

"I believe he visited some of the beautiful gardens of Italy, and they were the Callaway Gardens of his time."

Letting the balmy breeze dry the perspiration from our faces, for almost an hour we were silent and still. Out of the blue, Andrew came up with one of his zany zingers.

"Daddy, do you want to know why we have skulls?"

Prepared for an explanation that involved pirates, I confirmed that I did very much want to know the reason.

"Because brains are the mushiest part of our bodies and skulls protect our brains."

Indeed. "How did you know that?" I asked.

"Well, some things you just know. Nobody has to tell you," he said.

I heartily agreed that some things you just know. One thing I knew for sure was that the shared pleasures of our day at Callaway Gardens would provide fond memories for as long as the mushiest part of my anatomy continued to function.

Lightning in His Veins

I don't know the key to success, but the key to failure is trying to please everyone.

- Bill Cosby

Andrew wanted to talk about the courage of a young man we had seen earlier riding a bike with a prosthesis for a leg. Andrew was taken by the young man's mettle and determination. I didn't know the young man and couldn't elaborate on his life, but I told Andrew we could talk about another courageous person.

Lance Armstrong has led an inspiring and fascinating life. Books I've read indicate that Lance is an eternal optimist who believes that every obstacle is an opportunity. We talked about how Lance challenged and defeated one of the most deadly forms of cancer and went on to win the Tour de France bicycle race an unprecedented seven consecutive times.

The twentieth-century philosopher Rod Stewart in the song Rhythm of My Heart could be describing Lance when he sings about having lightning in his veins. A strong man who receives his share of criticism, some of which comes from small people who are envious of his remarkable accomplishments, Lance also knows how to love. He doesn't, however, confuse love with the need to stand for nothing in an attempt to be liked by everyone.

Even at age five, I see the spark of Lance's lightning in my son. The spark promises Andrew will become an extraordinary man.

The Liar's Dilemma

The secret of life lies in laughter and humility.

- G.K. Chesterton

Discussing what it takes to become a great athlete and a great person, and what it takes to survive life's many unavoidable challenges, I began describing Lance Armstrong's best character qualities – his preparation, determination and honesty.

"Daddy," Andrew said thoughtfully, "remember this morning when the lady at the restaurant asked if you wanted to buy the baseball cap? You said we bought one yesterday, but that wasn't true. You weren't being honest."

Andrew's words hit me like a freight train. "You're right," I said, struggling for a plausible explanation. "I just didn't want to hurt her feelings. Sometimes it's okay…"

Listening to my excuses, I decided to stop while I was behind. Changing gears, I said, "You're right, I told a lie."

"Daddy, you should have just said, 'No, thank you.'"

"I agree, son. I should have politely said no. Furthermore, I could tell the waitress knew I wasn't telling the truth."

She had hesitated before leaving the table. In the silence of her hesitation, I was afraid she was going to ask how much I had paid for the cap. I would have been forced to come clean or do what liars always do – lie to cover a lie.

It comes back to this: What we do must always support what we say. How confident can Andrew be in my admiration for Lance's honesty if I lie about little things like a baseball cap?

Laughing at the mental image of me ineptly fumbling for a price and thankful that the waitress had showed me mercy, I was nevertheless held accountable for not being truthful. We were not laughing about lying, but we did find levity in the liar's dilemma.

More than a Tire

Our last story of the day, shared in the quiet star-lit darkness of a country road, was about another form of courage. This time the courage was displayed by my Uncle Jim Whitney. After more than fifty years, the true account remains a vivid, important part of my life.

I was a little older than Andrew when I spent a week in Mobile, Alabama with Uncle Jim, Aunt Jane and my cousins, Micky and Kathy. Uncle Jim played professional baseball. Pleasantly personable with a big smile for everyone, he was a great husband, father and uncle. A deacon in his church, he lived his faith in matter-of-fact fashion.

One beautiful summer day I was in the car with Uncle Jim when we pulled onto a less-traveled country road. An elderly black man stood by the road, his time-worn Plymouth listing on a flat tire.

Stopping, Uncle Jim greeted him graciously. "Can I help you, sir?"

Attempting to assimilate the offer of assistance from a young white man in deeply segregated Alabama during the 1950s, the aged man paused for a moment, weighted by a lifetime of experiences. He answered that he didn't have a spare tire. Attempting to give my uncle an easy out, he added, "I don't have much money."

"I don't think we'll need any money. I think my spare will fit your car," said my uncle. Jim's Plymouth was a few years newer, but the tire did indeed fit. Jim did most of the work but the elderly man helped, and the car finally came down on its new spare tire.

When the work was finished, the handshake between the two men lasted a bit longer than usual. It was like the elderly man was buying time, searching for the right words. Still attempting to absorb the significance of the event, I could see the man knew it was about more than a tire.

Back then I had merely watched the interaction, too young to comprehend, but much later I understood that my Uncle Jim had been living the compassion and the courage of his Christian faith. He was setting an example for me to follow, helping me see what few others in Uncle Jim's time could see.

"What will I tell my wife?" the old man wondered. Uncle Jim's answer was simple, yet it provided a modern-day moral for Andrew to ponder.

"Just tell your wife that your brother Jim Whitney helped change your tire."

Chapter Sixteen

A LAND SPEED RECORD

A little comic relief in a discussion does no harm,
however serious the topic may be. In my own experience
the funniest things have occurred in the gravest and most
sincere conversations.

- C.S. Lewis

Biographies of meaningful people usually reveal that they enjoy conversations and reading. Successful families convey knowledge to their children with good books and stories. Presenting and re-inforcing value systems, legacies and fun through powerful stories is an excellent way to enrich our children's lives.

Mandy and I have read Andrew innumerable children's books, and he also enjoys the works of great literary composers such as Helen Steiner Rice, C.S. Lewis and G.K. Chesterton. These remarkable people were often self-effacing, yet they possessed an enriching perspective and sense of humor that gave them full sails.

Our standard bedtime routine includes stories about our own child-hood and about our imaginary characters, Paula Positive, Tommy Toyboy, Larry Liar and Harry Have-fun. These humorously concocted characters provide learning experiences about the virtues, vices and vicissitudes of life. Paula enthusiastically embraces life and likes gardening with her mom. Tommy is the material boy, always wanting more yet never satisfied. Larry offers a most valuable lesson: lies beget lies. Harry and his dad find fun in even the simplest events, including time spent in silence. Gradually we notice Tommy and Larry maturing and overcoming their vices with the help of parents, teachers and friends.

Watermelon Man

One evening I decided to tell Andrew a story that put his dad in a bad light. Admitting to our poor decisions doesn't encourage children to make bad choices, as long as they understand the unfavorable consequences.

For my seventeenth birthday my parents bought me a 1949 Plymouth. The thirteen-year-old car needed new tires, basic repairs and sprucing up, but for me and my friends it was a dream car. Dad decreed that our first priority would be to earn enough money to replace two bald tires. Until the new tires were secured, I could work on the car but not drive it.

Andrew asked how much two tires cost. I told him two weekly collections from my paper route and three or four lawn-cutting jobs would provide the necessary cash. I want Andrew to link work with what he wants from life, so I was heartened when he readily embraced the connection.

Knowing that sharing fun with friends enhances the experience, Andrew asked if my friends helped with the work. Only those who wanted to share the ride, I said. Bob, Roy, Stewart and I were delivering papers and cutting grass, and in between earning money for the tires we began fixing up the car that would set us free. Soon we would be free from the school bus and free from walking – and one step closer to the American dream.

We decided to paint the Plymouth. Choosing a bright pea green color and driving the car ten yards from the street to our carport, there was serious jockeying for shotgun position. Opening paint cans, we dipped our brushes and started converting the shabby black Plymouth into our bright green ticket to ride. We nicknamed the car the Melon, and I became the Watermelon Man.

I kind of liked being the Watermelon Man. That was the name of Mongo Santamaria's popular and catchy instrumental. The only lyrics were "Wa-ter-mel-lon Man," but it was one of those songs that just gets stuck in your head. Even now fragrant slices of watermelon evoke pleasant memories and start my toes tapping.

Our pea-green paint job was a fright, but we were pleased with our efforts. I believe the consensus was, "Well, it looks better than it did."

Delivering papers and cutting grass was hard work. As we slowly gathered the cash, Stewart came up with a less-expensive way to acquire the tires. Walking over to 27 Avenue, he observed that free pre-owned tires with good tread could be found at a nearby tire store. Hearing this, Andrew said, "Ding!"

This is our way of showing that we recognize a lie or wrong-doing in a story. Questioning the legitimacy of finding good tires at no cost, Andrew agreed that this fell into the category of *what sounds too good to be true is probably not true.*

"Dad, there are no free lunches," Andrew said with a smile.

The tire shop was closed, but Stewart was sure the owner wouldn't mind if we took a couple of used tires. Ding! I wanted to believe him, but a nagging voice in my head kept asking awkward questions. Why were the tires locked up? Finally admitting that Stewart was proposing we steal a couple of tires (ding!), I began to rationalize. After all, they were only used tires and the owner would hardly miss them (ding!). Stewart and I decided to go inside the enclosed truck (ding!) and look around. Covering the back of the vehicle was a cage made of chain-link fence. Stewart pulled up the bottom of the gate and I slipped under. As I squeezed into tire heaven, the heavy metal gate began hurting Stewart's hands. He let go, and the gate dropped with an ominous thud.

The infractions were coming so quickly that Andrew had stopped dinging and was just listening intently. The bottom of the gate fit dreadfully well into a groove on the truck floor. After many attempts to free the gate, I anxiously looked around. I was trapped, a bumbling pilferer. The truck would be my bedroom for the night.

We weren't through with our web of deception. There would be at least one more lie. Stewart needed to get home to be there when my mom called. He would tell my mom I was in the shower and that everything was okay for my sleepover.

I settled into my cell for the night. Only moments before I made such an effort to enter, but now I badly wanted to leave. I had plenty of time to reflect on how easily I had been led. I soon loathed the odor of tires, but they were less uncomfortable than the bare floor. Attempting to rest on a pile of stinking rubber in the round, I began cooking up a story about how I got stuck in the truck.

Pausing, I asked Andrew who was most wrong in attempting to steal the tires. After giving the matter some thought, he responded.

"Both of you!"

I confirmed his astute verdict. We agreed that attempting to hold someone else accountable for a poor decision is another poor decision.

It hadn't escaped Andrew that part of my penal sentence was the unenviable state of being "least uncomfortable." Amused but not in the least bit accepting of his dad's behavior, Andrew recognized that the lies and self-deception were mounting. But was I through with my deceptions?

"I finally decided I had done enough wrong," I confessed, much to his relief. "I would tell the truth with the rising of the sun."

The next morning when the owner arrived I summoned him. Angry, he confronted me about being in his truck. We talked, and I came clean. After assuring him that I'd learned my lesson and wanted to make restitution, he decided against calling the police. I offered to work for him for free after school and for the next few Saturdays. The owner was gruff, yet gracious. He said I did a good job, and let me work long enough to acquire the two tires I needed.

Telling Andrew that the Plymouth drove better on tires earned through honest labor, I confirmed that I had learned at least two valuable lessons from the experience. The first lesson was that honest labor is more rewarding than lying and stealing. Second, I did not want to change tires for a living.

Daydream Believer

> *The potential for greatness lives within each of us.*
>
> - *Wilma Rudolph*

Andrew's first venture in organized sports was playing basketball in the four- and five-year-old league at the Fowler Mill YMCA near our home. He made great strides in his round-ball abilities and learned how to listen to his coaches and interact with his teammates. He was proud of his reversible blue-on-white jersey although he did need reminding that he was wearing a uniform, not a costume.

His good friend, Jacob Pfundt, played on the same team. Mandy and I are friends with Jacob's parents, Charon and David. They live an easy walk from our home, and one night sitting on their comfortable front porch we talked and watched our boys playing for a couple of hours. It was Friday so we didn't mind the boys romping until close to 10 pm. After Andrew's bath he requested a story, but it was late and I decided in favor of Mozart. Andrew, however, had a specific plea.

"Please talk about the lady who couldn't walk."

I responded with the abbreviated version. One of my favorite stories, it is an improbable-but-inspiring account about the twentieth of twenty-two children. Learned medical professionals had told her parents that she would never walk, but the determined little girl had a dream and she realized her dream. At the 1960 Olympic Games in Rome, Wilma Rudolph ran her heart out and became the first American woman to win three gold medals in an Olympics.

"Never underestimate the power of dreams," I concluded my story for the evening.

Listening To Silence

Going to sleep with the heartwarming and inspiring story of Wilma Rudolph on his mind, Andrew had almost dozed off when he mentioned that his throat was bothering him. I gave him some over-the-counter medication and put vapor rub on his throat and chest.   He awoke around midnight with an ear-ache painful enough to warrant a trip to the emergency room at Joan Glancy Hospital. A nurse beckoned us and began asking me the usual questions.

"Is Andrew allergic to anything?" she wanted to know. Before I could respond, my son answered in a weary, pain-depleted voice.

"Oatmeal."

Andrew's ear-ache soon cleared up, to my great relief. I believe that making time to listen is a substantial beginning to effective communication. A child's spiritual, mental and physical growth should include time for listening, contemplation and meditation. For example, listen to this: it is an encounter between Mother Teresa and a reporter:

> *Reporter: "What do you say when you pray?"*
> *Mother Teresa: "I don't say anything. I listen."*
> *Reporter: "What does God say to you?"*
> *Mother Teresa: "He doesn't say anything. God listens. If you don't understand that, I can't explain it to you."*

Our culture places so much emphasis on talking it is small wonder that we struggle with the quieter aspects of communication.

On Being Creative

We encourage Andrew to reach out for life, to make his share of mistakes. What we do wrong confirms our nature and fosters the need for forgiveness. A meaningful life includes many failures. Perhaps the harshest failure is not trying, not making plans to succeed, and not having a vision.

Eating dinner on our porch one evening, Andrew asked for a second time to be excused to use the restroom. He stood, awkwardly carrying something in his left hand. Upon further inspection, his clandestine napkin-wrapped bundle betrayed a plot to ferry his unwanted okra to the toilet.

Explaining that in my own childhood I had also used the stuffed-napkin method, as well as the squirrel-cheek method, to dispose of unwanted vegetables, I revealed that my favorite ploy had been the under-the-plate ruse, which required volunteering to clean the table and was most effective if I also agreed to wash the dishes.

"If I didn't invent the ploy I perfected it," I chuckled after congratulating him on his inventive maneuver. "You may find it easier to eat what's on your plate."

Pensively, my son asked if he could possibly add okra to the list of foods to which he is allergic. He reminded me that he enjoys some vegetables, especially corn and broccoli. But when did macaroni and cheese become vegetables?

The Joy of Unselfish Giving

Many nights our bedtime routine highlights a particular composer or composition. In this manner we have come to better appreciate Pachelbel's *Canon*, Schubert's *Impromptu*, Mozart's *Divertimento* and Johan Strauss's *Wine, Woman and Song*. The nightly routine provides a remarkable opportunity to help convey the humor, joy and meaning of life. After fifteen to twenty minutes of stories, reading and focus music we usually end in prayer, often by thanking God for our special time together. We based last night's prayer on Helen Steiner Rice's poem, *The Joy of Unselfish Giving*, taken from her book, *And the Greatest of These is Love: Poems and Promises*.

Time is not measured
By the years that you live
But by the deeds that you do,
And the joy that you give –
And each day as it comes
Brings a chance to each one
To love to the fullest,
Leaving nothing undone
That would brighten the life

Or lighten the load
Of some weary traveler
Lost on Life's Road –

So what does it matter
How long we may live
If as long as we live
We unselfishly give.

- Helen Steiner Rice

Rocket Bus

I think we underestimate the importance of play. A lack of play undermines a person. We often relegate time for play to what is left over after everything else is done, but all too often there just isn't any time left over for fun. When is the last time you spent a day in play, a day filled with long, hearty, healing laughter?

After sharing dinner with my brother, Bob, his wife, Janie, and my nephew, David, who is a senior at Valdosta College, we all stayed at the table trading humorous memories. Bob is three years younger than me and Mary, my sister, is three years younger than Bob. We grew up in an FHA community just north of Miami that included modest homes, schools, churches and a nudist colony.

The nudist colony was surrounded by an eight-foot fence and mature Australian Pines. Many of us neighborhood boys had plans to stealthily enter the compound, but fear of the shotgun-toting guard outweighed our curiosity. One Saturday morning, however, a Miami-Dade patrol car entered our driveway with Bob in the back seat. It seems Bob's curiosity – or perhaps his hormones – had triumphed over his fear. Bob has remained mum about what he did or did not observe while trespassing at the nudist colony that day, and I'm pleased to report that he has had no further brushes with the law. After a successful career in banking, he retired early so that he and Janie could travel the world.

Telling tall tales about our childhood and some of our more-colorful escapades, Bob and I agreed that the person who had given us the most valuable direction, usually in the form of humor and play, was Uncle Lenton.

Uncle Lenton is a creative man with a great sense of humor. Back then there was no one better at telling a spooky bedtime story. His scary tales had all of Robert and Minnie Watson's grandchildren sleeping with one eye open on the summer nights we spent at their home in Newnan.

My favorite story involving Uncle Lenton happened when I was nine years old and about to take my first solo bus trip. My mom, siblings and I were in Newnan that summer at my grandparent's home when I was invited to visit a friend whose family had lived down the street from us in Miami before moving to Auburn, Alabama.

Billy Brown and I were good friends. For half the years of our lives we had gone to school together and played together. I looked forward to spending a week with Billy and his family including his beautiful teenage sister, Brenda, but it wasn't easy to get permission from my mother to ride alone on the bus.

Uncle Lenton intervened on my behalf. He accepted the responsibility taking me to the Greyhound station, and told my mother that he would personally ask the driver to confirm that the Browns had successfully gathered me in Auburn. With Uncle Lenton's commitment, permission was finally granted.

You'd have thought I was emigrating to the Antarctic. It was a radiant Saturday morning. I removed two precious dollars in change from the Prince Albert tobacco tin hidden under my grandparent's home, and after a round of hugs and well-wishes sprinkled with generous dollops of advice I began my first solo journey. At the bus station my gregarious Uncle Lenton confirmed my departure and arrival times and asked for a seat close to the driver. Sitting on an old bench, we went over what to expect.

"Here's your ticket, sport. You'll be sitting close to the driver and you'll have a great view. There will be a short stop in La Grange to let people off and on. Keep your seat, because if you get off in La Grange we may never see you again."

My playful uncle had a special manner of telling you what you needed to do without being dictatorial or condescending. He found fun in just about everything.

"The bus leaves at noon and gets into Auburn at 12:20 pm. Including the stop, that's seventy miles in twenty minutes. You'll be traveling at more than two hundred miles an hour in a Greyhound bus and breaking the world's land-speed record!"

Sitting at the dinner table, Andrew looked at me with bewilderment. I sympathized with his concern, having shared those same feelings many years before. But at that moment, the public address system announced the imminent departure of my rocket bus.

"Uncle Lenton, is the bus really going to go two hundred miles an hour? Will you stay until it leaves?"

"You bet, Nicky! If this thing is going to cover seventy miles in twenty minutes, I want to watch it blasting off!"

Uncle Lenton waited until the last possible second. As I reached the bus door, he finally explained that Alabama is in a different time zone, an hour behind Georgia.

It was an unforgettable lesson about time zones. Exchanging relieved smiles from my perch on the bus seat, I mentally wiped my brow. The wheels wouldn't be flying off my metallic pachyderm, but I nevertheless regretted missing the opportunity to be part of a world land-speed record.

When the bus departed I already felt a sense of accomplishment. It was sinking in. I was truly traveling on my own to another state, in another time zone. Riding the bus independently added to the excitement I felt over visiting Billy and the Brown family in another state. I just knew Brenda would be impressed when I swaggered off the bus alone. Boys of all ages are inspired and motivated by attractive women.

From the front row seat I had a terrific view of the countryside. Leaning over, the driver said that a nice lady would be sitting beside me at La Grange. Taking in the pastoral views of small-town America, I saw weathered stores with faded Coca-Cola, Sunbeam Bread and Prince Albert signs, fenced pastures with big bales of hay and small churches with expansive graveyards.

Pick 'Em Up, Molly

In La Grange a plump lady carefully climbed aboard the bus carrying a large shallow box almost as wide as it was long. Smiling, she managed the stairs with the help of the driver. I also offered a helping hand.

"Thank you, sugar," she said pleasantly.

Back on the highway, it was apparent that the lady and the driver were friends when they began talking about their respective families. Rounding a corner, the awkward box slipped from the lady's lap and careened to the floor. A small armada of chirping baby chicks escaped. As the yellow birds began scurrying every which way, the flustered woman went into action. Several of the chicks had fled for refuge into the stairwell. Bending down to retrieve them, she passed gas.

It was only loud enough to be audible to the operator and myself, but like most boys I found any noise emitted by the human body to be extremely funny. However, under the circumstances I hesitated to laugh. Not the driver, who erupted in laughter. Wiping the tears from his eyes he said, "Pick 'em up, Molly, don't shoot 'em."

Much to the surprise of Mr. and Mrs. Brown and the delight of Billy and Brenda, I arrived in Auburn cradling a soft, yellow chick in my hands. After my capable assistance rounding them up, Miss Molly had given me one, but neither of us had a suitable container. Confidently swaggering off the bus in anticipation of Brenda's admiration at my daring journey, my cavalier attitude was suddenly and considerably diminished. It's hard to be cool after a chirping chick poops in your hands.

Chapter Seventeen

SWEET HOME ALABAMA

God gave us memories that we might have roses in December.

- James M. Barrie

Rolling out of bed at five in the morning, Andrew rose without hesitation. This morning he was excited about catching the train. On our third Amtrak trip, our destination would be Anniston, Alabama.

I like *being* up in the early morning, not necessarily getting up. After groaning my way out of bed, the early-morning hour before dawn is one of my favorite times of day. Andrew, who shares my fondness for the wholesomeness of daybreak, was already brushing his teeth and pulling on his clothes.

"Let's go, Mom," he exhorted. "We don't want to be late!"

Mandy had agreed to drive us to Gainesville, where we'd have plenty of time to watch the Amtrak Crescent arriving at 7 am. Under the "kids ride free" fare on the Crescent, our total round-trip from Gainesville to Anniston cost only $78. On our way to Anniston, we'd go through Atlanta and be able to see the historic downtown areas of Buford, Duluth and Norcross. This time we would stop short of Andrew's birthplace in Birmingham, but there was much to do in Anniston.

Waving goodbye to a smiling Mandy in Gainesville, we boarded the train and made our way to the dining car. What could be better than viewing the world over an Amtrak breakfast?

Dawn unfolded with the expansive promise of a new day. We have been to Buford, Duluth and Norcross many times, but this time we were viewing these familiar places through the wide windows of a train. Our fond memories of frolicking in the Duluth fountains and playing in Thrasher Park in Norcross took on additional significance.

Swaying smoothly down the track, the familiar clickety-clack of the train wheels brought back memories of riding the rails when I was a boy. Back then I had been fascinated with train travel, and now it was obvious that my smiling son was enjoying this journey. Over breakfast, we gave thanks for all things big and small.

Assimilating the sights of Atlanta and passing lesser-known, but no less interesting, historic towns like Tallapoosa and Heflin, mesmerized by the passing forests and undulating open fields comprising the pastoral life of rural America, we returned a child's wave and felt a surging thrill at each whistle-blowing, bell-ringing, red-light-flashing crossing. We were experiencing Americana, having fun and appreciating the lives and times of so many other people, places and things. Our journey to Anniston was measured in minutes and decades – our ride, both nostalgic and edifying, brought grateful smiles to our faces. It was the best of times.

Looking out at the passing scenery, Andrew wanted confirmation that one day we would ride a train through the scenic Canadian Rockies and the Grand Canyon. Allaying his concerns, I affirmed that we had already started gathering information. We agreed that Mommy would come on these special trips.

Parents Needed: Wimps Need Not Apply

As we finished our breakfast a family of four sat down a couple of tables away. They had a son about Andrew's age who decided to run, yelling, up and down the aisle. The parents, when they even bothered to pay attention, merely asked him to sit down. As inducements they offered him a donut, and later a toy. They made several frail requests in twenty minutes, but the child paid little attention. Changing tactics, they counted to ten twice, but the child continued blatantly disturbing everyone in the dining car.

"Why didn't they just tell him to sit down and be quiet?" Andrew asked as we exchanged disbelieving glances. We felt bad about the disruption the rude family had wreaked on the other diners.

I am always taken aback and disappointed by parents who lack the courage to require the respect of their children. It is alarming to me that many parents don't demand that children who are acting disrespectfully knock it off, sit down and be quiet. Often these same parents lavish praise on their disruptive children for accomplishing little more than inhaling and taking up space. The inevitable partner of wimpy parents is misery. Caring comes from parents who dare to discipline.

Crapple

Descending the Amtrak Crescent in Anniston, we discovered that we had ridden back into an easier time. Walking the interesting mile from the modest Amtrak station to downtown, people smiled and greeted us warmly. After stopping to watch water rushing down a storm drain and to pet carefully a stray dog, we reached Main Street about mid-morning and sat on a bench swigging bottled water.

Watching cars and pedestrians pass, some with a friendly wave, we offered each other conjectures on their destinations. Andrew asked whether the urban hike from the train station to downtown was our exercise for the day. I assured him that our walk, along with some quality time in the Quality Inn's swimming pool, would satisfy our daily exercise goal.

Andrew already values fitness, nutrition and good health. Every morning his health drink consists of a fresh vegetable and fruit juice combination to which we often add flax seed or some other healthy fiber. Andrew's favorite blend is carrot and apple, but I am convinced that taste is not the only reason he likes the wholesome mixture we named Crapple.

An American Hero

Passing time waiting for our taxi to arrive, we began sharing jokes. "Did you hear about the couple whose purse and wallet were stolen while they were on vacation? They decided against reporting the loss of their credit cards – the thief was spending less than them."

This joke started us talking about heartbreaking vices such as the misuse of debt. We discussed the importance of avoiding foolishness like lying, quitting, overeating, gambling, drugs, smoking, complaining, boasting, laziness, impulsive buying and credit card debt. Just about the time we realized the summer temperature was surpassing ninety, a lady approached us and suggested that we might find it more hospitable to wait for our cab in the air-conditioned lobby of the hotel behind us.

Gladly accepting her generous offer, we found ourselves in a turn-of-the-century hotel that had once been frequented by many famous folks, including a former president. We were even more appreciative of our cooler accommodations when a second call to the cab company indicated there would be further delay. It would be at least an hour before we'd be ferried to the Quality Inn in nearby Oxford.

Making good use of our lobby time, we inquired as to the name of the lady who had invited us in from the sweltering summer heat.

Gina Perez had recently lost everything, including her home, in hurricane Katrina. She was not bitter; instead, she was forgiving. After settling into her extended-stay hotel she had no desire to blame the gods, the president, nature or New Orleans officials. She was without negativity. Having lost everything, she doubted she'd return to New Orleans. She liked living in Anniston.

I was watching the empathy in Andrew's eyes, thinking how fortunate we were for this opportunity to spend time with Gina. Without pomp, she exemplified many of the positive characteristics that Mandy and I have prayed our child will embrace and apply in his own life. An hour passed, and our taxi arrived. Reluctant to leave the conversation, we wished our new friend well. In the taxi Andrew wanted to better comprehend Gina's ordeal so we talked further, and again that evening over dinner we discussed her situation. I assured Andrew that Gina would do well because she possessed at least four of life's essential qualities – courage, forgiveness, optimism and purpose.

Just Another Day in Paradise

At our motel, it didn't take long to escape the heat by plunging into the pool. I can't imagine anyone, or anything, with or without a fin, liking swimming more than Andrew.

Only the allure of watching the sunset from a mountaintop created enough interest to get him out of the pool.

Cheaha Mountain was a pleasant thirty-minute drive from our Quality Inn in Oxford. At the summit, the highest point in the state of Alabama, the Cheaha State Park Lodge restaurant offered expansively vibrant views of rolling evergreen and hardwood timberland. A beautiful lake far below the lodge's lofty perch sparkled in the setting sun as Andrew and I shared fresh trout and interesting conversation about Gina.

After dinner, there was still enough light for a good walk along the summit, following which we decided to return to the lodge for ice cream. On our way back, in the fading light Andrew miscalculated a jump from one boulder to the next and fell with a thud. Recovering, he said with a smile: "It's a good thing this ground is soft."

Our laughter was not because he had fallen, but because we felt good. It had been another day in paradise. Peacefully sitting on a large rock, breathing the sweet scent of evergreen and other enriching forest fragrances, we looked happily out over the rolling mountain range.

Lincoln International Speedway

A cup of ice cream, a pleasant drive, a prayer and a good night's sleep later, it was almost 9 am when we awoke cheerful and refreshed. I was in the bathroom shaving. Brushing his teeth, Andrew began humming *Happy Birthday.*

"Whose birthday is it?" I inquired.

"Mommy told me to brush my teeth for as long as it takes to hum *Happy Birthday* three times."

Hopping into our bright-red compact rental car, which Andrew quickly named the Tomato, we made our way to the Talladega Super Speedway. The racetrack is located in what appears to be Lincoln rather than Talladega, Alabama, but I suppose it's too late to call it the Lincoln International Speedway.

This observation cultivated a conversation about anomalies. I told Andrew that the New York Giants should more appropriately be named the New Jersey Giants because they play their home games in the Meadowlands Sports Complex located in East Rutherford,

New Jersey.

"Where is the Cincinnati International Airport?" I continued.

"I know it's not in Cincinnati," Andrew replied.

"It's not even in Ohio!" I said, congratulating my son on being observant. The airport is located in Kentucky. We decided to shelve our notion to rename the Talladega Super Speedway.

My friend, Lincoln Mayor Lew Watson, was a primary force in getting Honda Motor Co. to locate its production plant and many new jobs in Lincoln, a pleasant yet relatively obscure town located between Birmingham and Anniston. The mayor helped me get my employer SouthTrust Mortgage approved as Honda's mortgage lender of choice, and he introduced me to NASCAR's most competitive track. Many years before, the mayor had called the good folks at the speedway on my behalf and arranged a package tour of the International Motor Sports Hall of Fame. The package had included a drive around the storied Talladega Super Speedway. Now the mayor had again graciously arranged for a package tour, only this time it included my son.

Sheepishly driving the bright red Tomato into the hall of fame parking lot, we quickly abandoned our puny, distant cousin to the mighty racecars and spent about an hour in the hall of fame.

Saving the best for last, we made our way to the track. Speeding down the high-banked track in a real racecar, our guide told us heroic stories about racing legends. To keep them from launching into space, NASCAR requires restrictor plates on cars racing at Talladega. On the backstretch, where the high-performance cars exceed 200 mph, we imagined we were racing for the checkered flag beside Petty, Allison and Earnhardt. I found it all immensely exciting, but Andrew was surprisingly reserved until the end of the tour. Approaching the tunnel exiting the super speedway, he finally perked up.

"Daddy, look! A John Deere grader!"

With a top speed of twenty miles an hour and no restrictor plate, John Deere had trumped the mightiest designs of Ford, Chevy and Dodge.

What We See in Darkness

Nothing in the world can take the place of persistence. Talent will not; nothing is more common than unsuccessful men with talent. Genius will not; unrewarded genius is almost a proverb. Education will not; the world is full of educated derelicts. Persistence and determination alone are omnipotent. The slogan 'Press On' has solved and always will solve the problems of the human race.

- Calvin Coolidge

From the super speedway (or the John Deere grader, depending on your perspective), we traveled another thirty pleasant miles to Desoto Caverns Park near Childersburg, where we found cool respite inside a cave the size of a football field.

Gazing up twelve stories in some places and bending down in other places to pass through low openings, we explored the enormous cavern. A thought-provoking aspect of the tour occurred when our guide turned off all the lights. For a full minute, we experienced complete darkness. Our guide invited us to place our hands immediately in front of our faces to confirm that the cave was void of any light. This was a first for Andrew. He wanted to talk about the experience of complete darkness.

After seeing the Desoto Caverns, we visited a nearby amusement park with rides that Andrew enjoyed, then drove back to Oxford using our time in the car to talk about the blessings of our senses and the fortitude of those who don't have all their senses. Unfortunately, I could not adequately explain to Andrew why some of us seem to have all our senses, while some of us do not. I did, however, have an enduring example about courage in the face of physical adversity.

Helen Keller lived most of her fruitful life in Tuscumbia, a small city in the northwest part of Alabama a couple of hours drive from Memphis, Tennessee. I had visited her birthplace home, now preserved as a historic site, a few times. Sitting on a white bench in the well-maintained garden of her family home, it was rewarding to contemplate the incredible spirit of someone who had overcome the inability to hear, speak and see.

Helen Keller's story of courage was also the story of her incredible friendship with her teacher, Anne Sullivan. Andrew and I agreed that Helen Keller's life is a powerful testimony to faith, courage and persistence. She is an awe-inspiring person. What reasonable excuse do the rest of us have not to fulfill what God has planned for our lives? Andrew wanted to know more about the miracle worker so before returning to our motel we visited the Anniston public library, where we found this telling and inspiring quote:

On Herself

They took away what should have been my eyes,
(But I remembered Milton's Paradise).
They took away what should have been my ears,
(Beethoven came and wiped away my tears).
They took away what should have been my tongue,
(But I had talked with God when I was young.)
He would not let them take away my soul –
Possessing that, I still possess the whole.

                                        - Helen Keller

Chapter Eighteen

THE GOOD LIFE

Don't forget how great your family is; don't take them for granted; don't lose your temper when you should be calm; don't cry when you can laugh. Most of all, be grateful.

- Cameron Stracher

Celebration

Mandy wanted to celebrate the sixth anniversary of her thirty-ninth birthday on the coast, so we made plans to go to Savannah and to Tybee Island. One of our favorite weekend get-away places, Tybee has the closest beach to our home. We often go there when we want to be on the ocean.

For her birthday dinner, Mandy chose a family-owned Greek restaurant on the Savannah wharf and we reserved a table overlooking the deep, wide Savannah River. Mandy wanted to shop for a couple of hours before dinner while Andrew and I decided to ride the complementary Westin and Marriot hotel water taxis.

Both boats are large, nicely appointed and air-conditioned – more like water limos. The taxis provide interesting visual perspectives of the river and the historic Savannah wharf. We watched cargo ships from all over the world entering the busy Savannah Port. I told Andrew that it was not a good sign for our county that the ships arrived heavily laden but departed high in the water.

In the restaurant sitting at our waterfront table and watching the activity on the river, we shared the house specialty of whole grouper and trimmings. At the end of the dinner a chorus of singing waiters surprised Mandy with a birthday cake. It was a wonderful dinner celebration and Mandy loved every minute – except for one incident.

"Did they have cars when you were little or just horses?" Andrew asked his age-conscious mother.

My forty-five – er, thirty-nine-year-old wife and I shared a laugh imagining what he might ask at my next birthday. "Dad, have you always walked upright, or did you start out on all fours?"

It was still daylight as we drove fifteen miles from Savannah to Tybee Island. Checking into our motel, we quickly donned bathing suits and made our way to the beach to work off some of our scrumptious dinner – whether upright or on all fours. With the sun setting behind us and the nearly full moon replacing it, we welcomed the pleasant ocean breezes and the warm surf splashing over our feet. We gave thanks in celebration of Mandy's birthday and the wonders of life.

Everyone Loves a Parade

If there is anything we wish to change in the child, we should first examine it and see whether it is not something that could better be changed in ourselves.
                                        - Carl G. Jung

During three days on the shore including an additional day on Hilton Head Island less than an hour up the coast in neighboring

South Carolina, we built sand castles, swam, sang, ate well and enjoyed a dolphin-tour boat ride. On the drive home, we agreed to make one last stop.

Beaufort is just thirty minutes north of Hilton Head. Anticipating lunch on Beaufort's beautiful bay and approaching the marina, traffic started backing up. Impatiently I decided to avoid the congestion by taking side streets to the marina. Ironically, on the radio Dwight Yokum was singing *A Thousand Miles from Nowhere.*

"He sounds really lost," said Andrew.

I know the feeling, I thought, ruefully confident that during my lifetime of taking shortcuts I have driven an additional thirty thousand miles. The better example I want for Andrew would include looking at maps, following directions and even occasionally turning around.

Seeking an avenue to reach the marina, we encountered police barricades at the end of the first four intersections but at the fifth we found access. Anticipating a shortcut to our lunch we swiftly entered the unobstructed opening only to realize we had to turn right instead of left. Quickly negotiating the obligatory turn, we found ourselves squeezed between two sets of lively Masons, one set whirling around on miniature motorcycles in front and the other set zig-zagging behind us in tiny cars.

"We're in a parade!"

Mandy was astonished. Even after twelve years of marriage I could still manage to surprise my wide-eyed wife.

"Now what do we do?"

"The obvious, my dear," I grinned. "Smile and wave."
Mandy lowered her window and with a nervous smile started waving. Anticipating calamity, Andrew just sunk lower in his seat. His

head below the level of the window, he said in a dispirited voice, "I've never been so embarrassed."

During the time we have owned our nondescript white Grand Marquis it has been mistaken for a Norfolk Southern supervisor's car, a police car and a taxi, but there is no telling who the good people of Beaufort thought we were that day. Nevertheless, they kindly greeted us with smiles and waves, and for six blocks we continued participating in the parade, waving at all the happy people and several police officers. Finally discovering an opening, we departed the fanfare just as my cell phone rang. It was Dawn.

"Where are you?" she asked, hearing all the noise.

"You won't believe it!" I began, then stopped. Dawn is, after all, my eldest daughter. Laughingly telling her about our adventure, in my mind's eye I could see her rolling her eyes. Based on years of experience, Dawn gave her brother some sisterly advice.

"Get used to it – it makes for great memories!"

Parking, we walked several blocks to the downtown marina where the festival was in full swing. Settling in for lunch and a pleasing panoramic view of the marina, bay and intra-coastal waterway, we watched boats of many dimensions, some moored and some moving. Thankful that we had shared in the friendly South Carolina celebration, we savored our meal and the day.

After lunch crossing the bridge to Lady's Island and then another bridge spanning the inter-coastal waterway, the two spans furnished additional spectacular views of the splendid waterways teaming with vessels. We were on Highway 17, taking a circuitous route to avoid traffic. Predictably, Andrew asked how long it would take to get home. Four hours, I told him, pleased that he is learning to tell time properly but a little misty because not so very long ago I would have said we were eight kid shows from home.

More than Happy

"Why do people say they are making a left-hand turn rather than just a left turn?" I asked Andrew, fending off travel monotony. "Why not a left-foot turn, or a left-ear turn, or a left-eye turn? "Why do we say first of all, rather than merely first? When is first not first of all?"

Andrew stayed with me, but Mandy quickly lost interest and dozed off.

"What does it mean when people close a letter with more than happy? What is your understanding about the state of more than happy?"

Laughing, Andrew listened to a few more observations on life's anomalies before he too nodded off for a nap. So much for my career as a comedian, I thought. Driving down the highway, in the quietness of the car I began praying once again for more times like the weekend we had just shared. So far my cancer had not returned but I knew it could, and I wanted very much to savor every precious minute with my family. I had grown to better understand the opportunity and responsibility of being a father. It was especially important to lead by example. Two unwanted situations led to an interesting journey that brought meaning to the lives of a father and son and those around them. In fellowship, fun and frolic we unfolded the secret of life.

Rolling into our driveway in just under eight kid shows, I woke my travel-mates and we unloaded the car. Setting the last of our bags in the breezeway between garage and house, we paused to look through the evergreen and deciduous trees to the pleasing view of our lake, sharing a couple of minutes in reverent silence.

"I really like travel, but I like being home more-better," said Andrew. Recalling lazy summer afternoons diving from the dock and rainy nights just hanging out on our porch, watching the mallards foraging around the shoreline and a formation of honking geese flying over our boathouse, I tried to think of a suitable reply. A light breeze picked up the fragrance of jasmine, gardenia and rose, a most pleasing bouquet.

"We will live longer having filled our lungs with the pleasurable bouquets of nature," I began. "Life will bring many good times and some bad, but it is our challenge to find meaning even in what appears to be bad. We can savor the good times – especially those with family and friends. Andrew, I agree. Being home is more-better."

Living in the Promised Land

Celebrate your success. Find some humor in your failures. Don't take yourself so seriously. Loosen up, and everybody around you will loosen up. Have fun.

- Sam Walton

By all accounts Sam Walton loved God, country and family, including his Wal-Mart associates. He enjoyed his old truck, hunting, his bird dog and Moon Pies. Reading from *Sam Walton: Made in America*, that night at bedtime Andrew and I began discussing Mr. Walton's Ten Rules for Building a Business.

One of these edifying rules in particular caught our attention. Rule Six has relevance to all aspects of a successful life. In Rule Six Mr. Walton advises us not to take ourselves so seriously. Loosen up and have fun, he says.

Andrew's favorite bedtime tale about Mr. Walton occurred more than fifteen years ago when I was flying from Manhattan to Atlanta. We call it The Billionaire Who Liked the Simple Life. My associate and I were boarding a plane at La Guardia airport. Taking our seats, Tim asked if I had seen who was sitting in front of us. I hadn't. When I looked up, I saw the richest man in the world sitting a few rows ahead of us in coach.

A few years after seeing Sam Walton on the Atlanta-bound plane, I was flying to Dallas from Ft. Lauderdale. Delta had upgraded me from coach to first class, where I found myself sitting next to a kindly giant of a man – yards of arms and legs folded into a seat measured in inches. As the flight attendant offered beverages, the man and I started a conversation.

He was returning from fulfilling one of his life-long goals of fishing in the Florida Keys. In his early sixties, he had worked for Wal-Mart from the early days. A "greeter" who never sold one share of the company stock awarded him for his years of dedicated service; he retired a millionaire or, more precisely, a multi-millionaire. In no way boasting, he meekly told me he was now living his dream.

"What was Sam Walton like?" I asked. Andrew was very much interested in his answer.

"Let me think about that," the man said. Mr. Walton had passed away earlier that year. It was apparent that my seatmate still strongly felt the loss. After a few minutes of silence, I began to think that he would not answer.

"Sam Walton could run with the big boys on Wall Street," he finally said, "but he never lost touch with little people like me. I met him several times, and every time he made me feel special. He made work fun. He made life fun."

I found it interesting that the multi-millionaire mountain of a man beside me still thought of himself as a little guy. It appeared that humility added to the joy of his life.

Hard of Hearing

Later that evening as Mandy and Andrew slept I checked email and found one from my daughter Dawn's lifelong friend, Kim. The two girls have been close since kindergarten, and Kim is like a third daughter to me. She and her family still live in South Florida, where both my daughters were born and raised.

I am grateful for my relationship with my children's friends. Fathering is about giving direction: take your vitamins, do your homework, clean your room, be a good citizen. It is about asking for forgiveness when we have failed. And fortunately, it is also about good times, laughter and the easier side of life.

Kim, Dawn and my nephew, Steven, had recently shared dinner where it appeared that my name had come up. Kim decided several years ago that our relationship had moved past Mr. Lore. While it was awkward at first now I'm okay with it, although I didn't check with Ann Landers or anything, and she addresses all her emails in the same way.

Hi Nick,

Dawn, Steven and I were reminiscing about good ole Nick Lore over pizza last week when Dawn was down visiting. We talked about Hal's restaurant where you often brought us kids for breakfast. We all had memories. One of mine was about the morning I left the table long enough for you to tell the server I was hard of hearing, particularly in my left ear. I remember she kept clumsily positioning herself to yell into my right ear.

We also recalled screaming when you showed up at one of our birthday parties in a gorilla suit. We had great memories of your semi-annual visits to the children's hospital ward for terminally ill kids dressed as Miss Piggy for Halloween and as Santa for Christmas.

We had many more fond remembrances that made us laugh. We talked about how we carry on your legacy and use these same bonding shenanigans with our own children.

Kim

A Costly Extract

Tommy Toyboy is Andrew's favorite imaginary character. Tommy and his parents struggle with the blessings and maladies of affluence. Tommy's collection of toys is legendary. With all the trappings of success including homes, cars and memberships, Tommy's parents provide him with more and more stuff, but this only leads to his insatiable desire for more. For the Toyboy family, contentment is ever-elusive.

Our imaginary characters offer insights for successful living. Some show life from a positive perspective, while others need help. Our characters often cross paths and offer each other help. Andrew listens searchingly, and the questions he asks help determine the course of our chronicle.

After telling him that we are blessed with many things in our country and that we all struggle with what to do with our abundance, one day while shopping in a health-food store he put me to the test.

We occasionally put a little lavender or eucalyptus oil on a cloth and place the fabric on our reading stand so we can inhale the pleasing aroma. It favorably adds to our reading and listening enjoyment. In the store we came upon a display of essential oils. While sniffing a few of the costly extracts, I said that perhaps we could add an additional fragrance to our collection.

"Daddy, don't you think that's being like Tommy Toyboy?" Andrew asked.

How many extracts are enough? Wisely, we decided to move on to the other items on our list.

Chapter Nineteen

MARIN COUNTY BILL OF RIGHTS

We never cared about money. Far more important than being rich is family and friends.

- David Gold

Driving an RV like an ATV

It was another easy Sunday afternoon with a houseful of family and friends sitting around looking like a Norman Rockwell painting. We'd just come in from a day on the lake, laughing and chatting. At dinner, my daughter Kimberly began reminiscing about a memorable vacation we had taken some twenty-five years earlier.

"Before the movies *Vacation* with Chevy Chase and *RV* with Robin Williams," she jovially mused, "there was my dad."

Dawn, Kimberly and I had left Miami for three adventurous weeks exploring in our twenty-four-foot rented travel home. We were headed for the Georgia mountains, our nation's capital, New York City and parts of Canada. On the first day at the intersection of two gravel roads, we stopped at a country store and bought snacks for lunch. The congenial owner shared the location of his favorite black-berry patch. He said he had picked berries there since childhood.

Almost there but not knowing it, we stopped for directions at a log home. A friendly couple explained that the blackberry patch was only a half mile ahead at the bottom of a hill. Soon we were at the top of a steep hill surveying the enticing expanse of brambles below. Putting the RV in gear, we slowly inched forward. The hill was steeper than it looked. Picking up speed, we slipped and slid to the bottom. Breathing a collective sigh of relief, we regarded the colossal patch brimming with beautiful, ripe blackberries.

"Let's get pickin!"

After a fun afternoon avoiding bees and filling our buckets (and mouths) with sweet, plump berries, we decided to return to Helen, Georgia, where we anticipated a tube run on the Chattahoochee River. Cranking up the motor home, we made an effort to regain the hill. Halfway up, the motor stalled. Backing perilously down, we tried again. Several attempts later, it was dishearteningly apparent that our RV was too top-heavy and underpowered to negotiate the steep dirt incline.

Walking back to the log home, we asked the kindly couple for the use of their telephone. They offered to let Dawn and Kim stay with them while I waited for a tow truck. Two drivers arrived and left, unable to assist. The last suggested he knew of only one person who might have the equipment to bail us out of our predicament. From the top of the hill, the third driver incredulously surveyed our situation.

"Did you drive down there on purpose?" he asked. I realized it was more an indictment than a question

"The only chance I got of getting you out is with my largest wrecker, which I have to bring up from Atlanta," he announced.

I could hear the cash register ringing, but we were in no position to negotiate. Two hours later he returned with a monster of a contraption. I'd never seen anything like it. It was spectacle enough that Dawn and Kimberly returned with the country couple to witness the wrecker in action. Looking down at the RV and then at me, the operator again voiced his disdain

"In all my years I never seen nobody do somethin' this stupid!"

We needed his help. Remaining prudently silent, I assumed he was right. Distress soon turned to elation as the sarcastic but skilled operator purposefully winched our rented travel home safely up the incline. We celebrated as the man collected his fee and left without fanfare.

Later that evening, calculating the price of our day's harvest, we determined the berries had cost $75 a pound. We also reflected on whether "never seen nobody" meant I wasn't stupid after all.

In the laughter around our dinner table when Kimberly finished her story, we began discussing that long-ago day. At first I had felt that it was a bad day. Part of me wanted to be disappointed. I had worried the girls. We had spent five frustrating hours attempting to get the RV up the hill. It had cost a lot of money, and I had become resigned to returning to the rental lot with nothing but the RV keys in my pocket. The experience had left me feeling like a turtle on his back.

Dawn offered a different perspective.

"I was concerned," she said, "but we had far more fun than worry. We met some great people, spent time together in the country and picked our fill of our favorite berry."

"I'll never forget that huge wrecker," Kimberly chimed in, grinning. It was gratifying to me that both girls had seen more good than bad in the day. They were right to point out the nice people we had met, and the fun we had, despite the difficulties. Robinson Crusoe didn't appreciate the beauty of a Caribbean paradise until he finally succeeded in escaping it, but Crusoe later came to appreciate the importance of embracing life on a daily basis. Successful people make plans and set goals, but they also make the best of their circumstances.

Choosing To Be the Best

One of the most difficult things I have ever done was telling Dawn and Kimberly at ages nine and six that their mother and I were getting divorced. That our marriage, and our family, had come to this was devastating. It was an excruciatingly difficult time, especially for the girls.

They were in the difficult position of deciding which parent to live with. After months of ugly legal wrangling, the court awarded me primary care of the girls with generous visiting rights for Dianne. It was a merely adequate solution in a hurtful situation.

One night soon after the divorce, sitting in our penthouse condominium overlooking the Emerald Hills golf course in Hollywood, Florida, I couldn't sleep. Inexplicably I emptied my wallet and briefcase of a dozen platinum, gold and diamond credit cards along with my country club membership card, my frequent flier card and my business card where below my name, embossed in gold ink, was the word President.

I was thinking that in the morning I would confidently don my gold watch and one of my tailor-made suits, lace up my Bally shoes and drive my Jaguar to work. I'd spend twelve or fourteen hours making important decisions and a lot of money. But I wouldn't be happy. Despite the power and respect – the success – that came with my position, I was disillusioned. My premium frequent flier and hotel cards were proof I'd been away from home too much.

The power of my position would eventually pass to someone else. I understood that most of my friendships – like those of Archie Smith in England – would follow the job. I was thankful for my lucrative career, but I questioned the wisdom of working such long hours and traveling so frequently, of being away from home so much. I wondered why I'd pushed Archie's advice so far back into the recesses of my mind.

After pondering things for a few weeks, I resigned my job of twelve years and took a position paying considerably less money, a job that allowed me to remain closer to home and to the girls' school. With minimal travel requirements from now on, most nights I'd be able to have dinner with Dawn and Kimberly. I would have more time for basketball games, recitals and performances. I felt fortunate that the girls still wanted me involved in their lives, and I didn't want to disappoint them like I had their mother.

Children don't issue gold cards, but they do recognize important positions. I had traded an important position labeled with the word president for an even more important position designated by an even more special word: "Daddy."

Sitting in the park after visiting the cancer clinic more than a year ago, my failed marriage and the pain it caused everyone had been uppermost in my thoughts. It was partly behind my decision to abandon a thirty-year career in mortgage banking to spend more time with my son. Now my fifteen-month adventure with Andrew was ending. Had I done the right thing?

I remembered another occasion that had strongly influenced my decision. Mandy and Andrew had joined me at a company picnic where my associates had hung a piñata for the children to whack. Most of the kids were a few years older than Andrew, who was watching with interest from the comfort of my lap. After numerous smacks, the piñata stubbornly held together. In frustration, one of the women said, "Come on, Mr. Lore, take a hit."

Wanting to be a good sport, I accepted. Realizing the candy-filled donkey was poised to burst after so much abuse and knowing my son was expectantly watching, I gripped the stick firmly and aggressively struck the hapless paper creature. It exploded with a spray of treats and Andrew, who had been studying the donkey's ordeal, ran to me. Excitedly he said, "Daddy, you're the best!"

Sitting on the park bench after my visit to the clinic, reflecting on the wisdom of prioritizing time, I had realized something profound. More than all of the pay and perks, I wanted to earn the respect of my children and bask in the joy of being a good dad.

Wealthy in Many Ways

In my own childhood, it didn't register with me that our family was economically lower middle class. My first clue came early in high school while dating a young lady whose parents had a large home in a prestigious community complete with luxury cars and other signs of success.

Even after realizing we weren't financially well off, I still felt fortunate. Both my parents were born into large, loving families. Both left grade school to help financially. Dad worked hard as a plasterer and did the best he could for his family. I always felt it was good enough. Mom, like most women of her time, was a homemaker. She kept a good house and made even the simplest of meals special. Our modest FHA home was where we belonged. We felt cared for.

In hindsight, we were wealthy in many ways. Dad didn't have the means to provide a college education for his kids, but he encouraged us to value education. Our parents often showed they loved us and told us that God loved us. Nothing is more comforting to children than knowing God and their parents love them.

We ate most of our meals as a family, often catching up on each other's news over dinner. Weekends and vacations were mostly simple but they, too, were family-oriented. Our first television had only one channel – we spent a lot more time outside playing with friends than inside watching television. When Mom sometimes had enough of us she'd say, "Go outside and play, and don't come back until I call you."

We'd go out and play, and then eventually she'd call. Those were good times.

What Matters Most

As a young man I met some of the wealthiest people in the world and found that they were such unhappy, lonely people. I learned that money and happiness are unrelated.

-Ross Perot

J.B. Fuqua had graciously accepted my invitation to lunch. I brought with me a copy of *Fuqua, a Memoir: How I Made My Fortune Using Other People's Money* so he could sign it for Andrew. Fuqua's book and good books like *Eat Mor Chikin: Inspire More People* by S. Truett Cathy will one day be must-reading for my son.

Mr. Fuqua's failing hearing made conversation difficult. Having for years encouraged this humble mega-millionaire to write his memoirs, I told him I felt it was a great book, but I still had some questions. I asked what he might have done differently with his life.

He said he would have relaxed and played more. He told me his biggest disappointment was the death of his son, Alan, at age eighteen. His greatest joys were his wife, Dorothy, and his son, Rex. He said family is what matters most. I asked Mr. Fuqua if he felt great wealth like his brought happiness.
"No," he said simply. We sat quietly for a while, and then he elaborated.

"I've met many substantially wealthy people in my life and I've read about others. I don't believe there is any correlation between great wealth and happiness. Surely a family that has enough money for a home and the basic provisions of life is happier than a family who doesn't. But the super wealthy often have more problems than a middle-class family. Great wealth often brings distractions and complications."

Mr. Fuqua was in every measure an American hero – my conversations with him were among the most memorable of my life. I didn't realize it then, but our lunch together was the last time we would visit. He died at the age of eighty-eight in April, 2006.

A Father-and-Son Cut

Andrew enjoys Saturday morning tooling around in our thirty-something-year-old Ford Mustang, especially when we go for haircuts. One Saturday on our way to get our ears lowered my five-year-old said he thought he was old enough to choose his own hairstyle.

At the barbershop, Andrew let me go first. When another barber became available, Andrew hopped in her chair. Looking at me, she asked about the cut. When I told her that Andrew was old enough to choose his own style, I could see his self-esteem rising.

"Andrew, how do you want your hair cut?" she inquired. Almost out of my hearing, his answer was composed and quiet.

"Just like my dad."

When we returned to the car, I turned and looked at Andrew.

"Why are you smiling, Dad?" he asked.

"Well, you chose a really nice haircut."

Laughing, we put the top down and shared an invigorating ride to the park. Bolstered by his experience in the barbershop, Andrew wanted to know when he could make more decisions about where we eat. That one was easy.

"When you buy."

A Million or More

For a few months, Andrew wanted to be a garbage collector. It was not our first career choice for our son, but Mandy and I never discouraged him. We told him the value of a person is in his character. We also shared our belief in the virtue of honest work, including garbage collecting. Nevertheless, we quietly rejoiced when one evening over dinner he announced that he had decided instead to become a train engineer.

Andrew is growing up in a world where even the government encourages him to gamble so that he may become an instant millionaire. The truth is that there are far more important qualities for a successful life including having faith, a good family and friends, an enjoyable career and personal character. Every day we see evidence that having lots of stuff is not the answer.

We are thankful that our son is already starting to understand this. Our fictitious characters provide lessons on the value of a positive attitude, on contentment, and on integrity. We have no stories where meaning is found in having millions of dollars. A million or more can change your life, but only occasionally for the better.

We encourage Andrew to look at our consumer-propelled society with a healthy skepticism, and to realize that often a significant chasm exists between worldly success and significance. The first measured in fame and fortune, while the latter – significance – is measured in moral and spiritual values.

Our special father-son journey would soon arrive at the door of kindergarten. For fifteen months we'd bonded in the light of laughter and adventure, but it would soon be time to settle into the excitement of a more formal learning process.

I remember headmaster De Ann Crawford asking me in an application interview who is most responsible for a child's education. The question underscored the responsibility and opportunity we have as parents. Parents have so much more occasion to instruct than any other institution in society. We also have the strongest motivation. This is why meals, play, rest, bedtime and just hanging out are so important. We can use these times as opportunities for learning.

Quality vs. Quantity

Years ago during a business dinner in San Francisco, the executive of a large California savings bank and his wife encouraged me to forsake my Friday-night redeye back to Florida. They had a second home in the Napa Valley and they wanted me to spend the weekend with them.

They were right in assuming I could easily rebook my flight for Monday. California's beautiful wine country is one of my favorite places in the world. I enjoyed their company and was tempted by their invitation, but I reminded them that as a single parent I needed to get home. I wanted to spend the weekend with Dawn and Kimberly.

This led to an extended conversation about parental responsibility. My emancipated associates, whose primary home was across the Golden Gate Bridge in Sausalito, subscribed to what they called a quality-versus-quantity parenting philosophy. According to this Marin County philosophy, whenever enlightened parents were away pursuing their dreams, older siblings, other caretakers and schools would step in to provide the required oversight of their children. They proposed quality of life over quantity of life, as if one could have quality without quantity in a loving relationship. I later dubbed this the *Marin County Parent Bill of Rights*.

My seat on the redeye was in an empty middle row. Stretching out for the long flight home, sleep eluded me. Pondering my dinner conversation, I was again thankful for my own committed and loving parents.

I believe the Marin County notion was innovative yet fallacious. It was a harbinger of some of the self-centeredness unhappiness of today. Men and women have every right to put themselves before parenting so long as they delay, or don't have, children. Once you have children, it seemed to me then and still does, you have a responsibility and opportunity of significant magnitude. The challenge of seeking a quality life for oneself without making time for our loved ones doesn't play well with children. The best way to get a kid to clam up is to only occasionally make time for him and then say, "Let's talk."

Flying High

Courage is rightly esteemed the first of human qualities because it is the quality which guarantees all others.

- Winston Churchill

Most days Andrew quickly makes friends in the park. I am content to perform my quiet feat of reading with one eye while keeping the other eye on the action. You may have noticed that five-year-olds are in constant motion.

One day, however, a boy somewhat older than Andrew approached and attempted to take his swing from him. Andrew looked puzzled, but held his ground. A tussle ensued. Leaving my park bench, I told the young man that Andrew was there first. I said that he needed to wait his turn. The boy made a derogatory comment, then ran off crying to his father.

The father and I spoke. I told him that I'd have done the same thing if our son's roles had been reversed. Satisfied, he apologized and we prepared to go our separate ways. As we parted, hoping to earn the potty-mouth kid a little time-out, I commented, "Contrary to what your son just said to me, I am not a stupid nerd."

On the way home, Andrew asked if I thought the boy had any friends. I replied that the boy was probably just having a bad day, and that he likely did have some friends. I also reminded Andrew that the measure of a man is found in his friends and in his foes. The person with a few friends is fortunate, while one with many friends is likely deceived.

Andrew asked why I had intervened in their scuffle over the swing.

"First, because I love you," I said. "Second, he was wrong and I wanted to offer guidance about what to do when someone is being unfair."

"Dad, I wasn't going to give him the swing," Andrew spoke with conviction.

"I know, son, and I admire your courage," I said. After a couple of minutes I quietly added, "I'm very glad you're my son."

Chapter Twenty

LESSONS FOR LIFE

Listen, my father, and you shall hear Harry Chapin's
foreboding warning in your ear.

- Nick Lore

This story about my children and me is also, and more importantly, a story about the marginalized role of fathers in families. The need for fathers, even one as flawed as me, to step up and be counted, to be regularly involved in the lives of their children, is substantial and urgent.

What children learn at school and church is important, but most of what I know today I learned before and after school. This is why fathers are so crucially important, especially for their sons. They need to see us living what they are learning, if we are to make a difference in their lives.

If you have young children, it is imperative to get started right now. If your children are nearly grown, you will need lots of celestial help. If you have what appears to be a fatally flawed relationship with your child, take hope by adopting an eternal perspective. Only the pride of an unrepentant soul is hopeless. A renewed relationship usually starts with a heartfelt apology. I can't bring myself to say that it is never too late, but I do believe that all things are possible with God. I do believe in miracles. We can all find hope in one of the incredibly wonderful aspects of God – He is not confined by time or space.

That's worth pondering. God is not confined by time or space.

If we want to heal the wounds, to be able to forgive, turn the hurt over to the Lord and move on, we must spare our children the pain of indifference. It starts with a game of catch, a story or dinner.

Dangerous Breakfast

One beautiful Saturday morning we were sitting down to fresh-from-the-garden blueberries on cereal when the doorbell rang. Mandy opened the door, and Matthew Williamson strode past her wearing safety pads and a helmet. With his skateboard tucked under his arm, he was clearly ready for the boy's skate-date.

Mandy and Matthew's mom, Sharon, remained in the foyer talking while I prepared him a bowl of berries and Wheaties. Staring at his friend's safety pads and helmet, Andrew began smiling broadly.

"What?" I asked.

"Must be dangerous cereal!"

God in the Dock

I know we have won many a soul through pleasure. All the same, it is His invention, not ours. He (God) made the pleasures: all our research so far has not enabled us to produce one.

-C.S. Lewis
(*The Screwtape Letters*)

The man sitting next to me was anxious and angry. It was a week since we'd both been diagnosed with prostate cancer, and now in the early-morning quiet of the RC Cancer Centers, waiting for our doctors to explain our options for therapy, the man was bewildered by his situation.

"How could He let this happen to me?"

A dozen years my junior, the man's question was directed at me but meant for God. It wasn't so much a question as an indictment. Replying only in thought, I felt empathy for the man – after all, we shared the same medical condition – but nowhere within me was the desire to blame God.

In recent months I'd realized that my prostate cancer had probably been caused months, if not years, before my diagnosis. I'd read enough to know that many years of stressful overwork, poor eating habits and neglecting time for proper rest and meditation was in great part the cause of my cancer. I didn't view the convergence of cancer and leaving my job as something God had done. Granddad Watson had told me that only good things come from God. I remained confident that he was right.

I am not one who has difficulty accepting the improbable. I am a product of the improbable. While an incomprehensible God is very much beyond my understanding, He is rather easy for me to believe in and accept. Any god that I can understand without faith is too little to be my God. I believe He makes time to involve Himself in even the seemingly ordinary things. I know He has in my life.

God has been a major part of my life ever since that day on the trestle when my faith was delivered by a southbound train. Growing up, he has been with me through a serious bout of Scarlet Fever, a congenital heart defect and my ADHD personality type that delights in pursuing peril. He was with me on the day I was diagnosed with cancer, and he was still there on that wonderful day fifteen months ago when I was declared cancer-free.

For the rest of my life, I must continue to return every six months for a PSA blood test. Any reading over 0.2 ng/ml will mean the cancer has returned. But the longer I stay cancer-free, the less chance there is that it will return. I have since had two more readings below 0.2 ng/ml. Ten years is a milestone where the doctors actually use the word cured. So is my faith stronger because God spared my life?

My faith is stronger because death has approached me and God has kept me from its reach. This is not the place for a spurious positive spin. For believers and agnostics alike, death is ugly and fraught with sorrow. It seems easier to cherish God when things are going our way, but the closer I've been to death the more I've believed.

I'm not suggesting that given the opportunity before death, everyone will accept God's gift of life. But as we near eternity, prideful lies and the posturing of self-absorbed fame and fortune hold no meaning. As we near death, there is no pretence. We either reach out for life, or futilely languish in the darkness and stench of desolation. There is no second place, there is no almost. There is only the starkest of distinctions between a resurrected life and the bleakest finality of death. I don't know if fire and brimstone are imagery or fact, but I do understand the difference between eternal love and abject hopelessness.

Apart from God, there is no love. Apart from God, there is no meaning. In Samuel Beckett's play *Waiting For Godot*, his hapless characters inertly wait for meaning to enter their barren lives. Godot, or meaning, never arrives. This is why I encourage Andrew to actively embrace God's purpose for his life – to find Godot!

Many things happened in the past fifteen months. For one thing, my faith grew stronger. Every day for the past fifteen months I thanked God for allowing me more time with family and friends, and especially for the opportunity to help Andrew mature into a man.

In my C.S. Lewis reading groups I ask the question: "What is the opposite of God?"

The usual answer is Satan, or evil, as if God has an equal, which, of course, He does not. There is no opposite. There is no equal to our Almighty God.

St. Augustine reminds us that God is, and always was, and always will be. Evil is nothing more than a parasite on good, tolerated by God but only for a while. God is the eternal truth and evil the finite lie that is exposed and soon will be forever banished. Satan, like a character in Greek mythology, knows the truth but is entangled in the web of his own lies, too prideful to humble himself to his Maker.

As we ended our odyssey and Andrew entered kindergarten, this is where it all came together for me. I am grateful to be able to believe. Every father's utmost responsibility is to accept this awesome gift and to help his children do the same by making quality time for them daily. The man who achieves worldly success yet fails his children has succeeded only in putting pearls on a pig. He has accomplished little of lasting value.

Fathers and Sons

After dropping an excited Andrew off for his first day of kindergarten, I returned home to sit meditatively watching the rain dancing on our lake. It was easier this time. He sort of knew what to expect, and he was excited about meeting his teacher and making new friends.

Once again, Mandy and I had let our son go. This time, however, I was grateful. We had shared a fifteen-month adventure. I had confirmed my belief that a good father-son relationship is important to the father, to the son, to the family and to society. I had also discovered that forging a strong father-son bond can stir up a great many memories.

This book about some of the people we met, the places we visited and the things we did is my humble attempt to preserve our adventure. In the telling of these stories I have attempted to also express the emotions, but passion is complex and difficult to convey. I suspect that the enduring strength of our father-son bond will be better appreciated from an eternal perspective.

As a role model for my children, I regret to admit that I am often found wanting. That's why in the manuscript I focused much attention on heroes and heroines – heroes not for who they are but for what they did, special for their virtues, especially in crisis. The battle is not about people, but about ideas and beliefs.

Not knowing if I would be around to pass them on personally to my son, I captured the most important of these ideas and beliefs in a list. It's not an exhaustive list of the life-lessons modeled by the special people we encountered during our adventurous fifteen months together, but the lessons we discussed most often. They are serving Andrew well as a child, and later on they will serve him well as a man. So for my son, and for everyone interested in living the rewarding life we were designed to live, here they are.

Andrew, when you embrace these lessons, they will become part of you. You will radiate with the goodness of the actions fostered by these beliefs. Just be diligent in remaining humble about what you receive. It is yours not to store, but to share:

1) Count your blessings with contentment. Listen, smile, laugh and give thanks often.

2) Prize above all else those who love you and wish you well. Decide who and what matters most, and prioritize your time accordingly. Avoid negative people.

3) Love your enemies. Praying for your enemies has the potential to change them, or you, for the better.

4) Respect others, and respect yourself. Respect is an essential virtue for a successful life, and self-respect is the foundation upon which all other forms are built.

5) Choose your friends with care, and make a great decision about who you marry. She must be right for you, and you must be right for her.

6) Live the courage of your convictions. The key to failure is trying to please everyone.

7) Keep the faith. Believing is seeing.

8) Avoid foolishness like lying, quitting, overeating, gambling, drugs, smoking, complaining, boasting, laziness, impulsive buying and credit card debt. Any one of these vices can ruin your life.

9) Dream. The potential for greatness lives within you. Examine yourself; discover where your true chance of greatness lies. Seize that chance and let no power or persuasion deter you.

10) Don't take yourself so seriously. Loosen up and have fun.

The Greatest Lesson

There is one more lesson; it is actually the first. When asked which is the greatest commandment or lesson, Jesus replied:

Love the Lord your God with all your heart and with all your soul, and with all your mind, and with all your strength... Love your neighbor as yourself. There is no commandment greater than these.

> *- Mark 12:30 & 31*
> *- Deuteronomy 6:5*

More Praise for

Roll the Windows Down, It's Raining

"A truly inspirational book from which every man, whether single, a father or grandfather, can gain valuable insights into Godly moral values and relationships. The volumes that Nick learned when faced with cancer, he shares freely so we can benefit and improve our own relationships. A must read for every man."

> - Richard J. Ackerman Sr., Facilities
> Coordinator, City of Snellville,GA

"… Underlying it all [Roll the Windows Down, It's Raining] is a deep spirituality that reminds us that we can seldom be our best on our own…."

> -Dr. James M. King, Pastor, Parkway Baptist
> Church, Duluth, Georgia

" *Roll the Windows Down, It's Raining* is a spirit filled father and son adventure. We get a glimpse into the lives of Nick and Andrew Lore and discover that it is through our loving father and son relationships that we know God."

> - Tracy Marshall, Columbia , SC

233

"Men today struggle to support their families not only financially but in other ways even more important. Amidst all the distractions and with little time, it is a real challenge to provide love and leadership in faith, compassion, wisdom, and strength. Nick Lore has walked that path and writes of what he's learned with humor and honesty. This book is the generous gift of his spirit, and his experience.

In reading it, I laughed; I cried; I emailed quotes from it to family and friends. I don't usually do that, but it was too good not to share."

- Lois D. Salter, Mayor of the City of
Berkeley Lake, GA

"Nick is a great story teller. As he recounts the adventures, we see just how God works with us through all situations in both the seemingly bad and good. We get to ride with him and Andrew as they take us on many journeys where God is at work. Everyone has a story, but few as gifted at telling it as Nick."

- Dr. Douglas Bell, DMA University of
South Carolina

"This book beautifully paints a colorful portrait of the cycles of life. It touchingly, meaningfully and profoundly ties one generation to the next, capturing both sweet and bitter moments. A true work of wisdom and Godliness!"

- Debbie Peters, Owner, Oak Grove Kids,
Lawrenceville, GA

"This is a must read book for all fathers and husbands. Nick has shared how to improve and enhance your family relationship and in that the meaning of life. He illustrates the way to find the joy of family and fatherhood through his story. My similar experience in life says Nick is right on target. His book can help anyone enrich their life and build strong family bonds."

-Thomas P. Spatola, President, Hardy Credit Co
Jacksonville, FL

LaVergne, TN USA
27 November 2010
206480LV00003B/123/P